HOLDING ON, LETTING GO

P 1 WEEK LOAN N

D0718770

HOLDING ON, LETTING GO

*Sex, Sexuality and People
with Learning Disabilities*

JOHN DRURY, LYNNE HUTCHINSON AND JON WRIGHT

A Condor Book
Souvenir Press (E&A) Ltd

First published 2000 by
Souvenir Press Ltd,
43 Great Russell Street, London WC1B 3PA

ISBN 0 285 63578 6

Typeset by Photoprint, Torquay, Devon

Printed in Great Britain by Creative Print and Design
Group (Wales), Ebbw Vale

Contents

Foreword

To get the best out of this book, please bear in mind the following points.

We use the word 'parent' throughout to indicate the main carer of the person with learning disabilities. The word 'carer' is used sparingly, as it can be confused with professionals such as care workers. Having talked to a number of people, we are comfortable with using the term 'person' or 'people with learning disabilities', while acknowledging that this, like many other terms, is subject to interpretation. When it comes to your child, your daughter or son, we have chosen to use all three of these ways of referring to them, whatever their age. Most of what we say relates to both children and adults, but where a point applies specifically to one or the other, we make that clear. The term 'learning disability' covers a whole range of people from those who have mild learning disabilities to those who have profound and multiple learning disabilities. We hope this book has some relevance to you whatever your situation

It may seem as though we are talking about people with learning disabilities as a homogenous group, when, of course, each person is a unique individual. However, the only way we have been able to approach the subject of sexuality and learning disability is to generalise. We trust that you will be able to take the general points we make and individualise them to your own situation.

People with learning disabilities are at the heart of all we say: they are the *raison d'être* of this book. However, since it is written for parents, it is you we are addressing. This whole subject is a complex one. Your views, experiences, hopes and fears are just one part of that. But, because we feel that not enough attention has been given to those views, we are concentrating primarily on you. Parents also are not a homogenous group: there will be as many differing opinions and experiences as there are numbers of people reading this book. So you may not agree with all we say, nor will all of it be relevant to you. We hope we are able to stimulate your thinking, give you some ideas for whatever next step you need to take, perhaps give you a sense of not being entirely alone, and encourage you to be part of a process that does make the lives of people with learning disabilities better.

Many people are becoming more aware of how complex the area of sexuality and learning disability is. Sexuality is a multi-faceted subject anyway: it touches all people, whether sexually active or not. It is integral to all our lives. By adding learning disability to the equation, with its issues of vulnerability, rights, protection and consent, the complexities deepen and multiply.

Clearly such a personal and complex subject as sexuality is marked and shaped by cultural, social and religious influences. Given what we've just said, we feel it is beyond the capacity of this book to deal with this added complexity. However, we hope we can provide some of the building blocks for widening the debate.

Some readers may feel that we are sidelining the rights of people with learning disabilities in favour of their parents' rights. To an extent this is true. Our work has led us to understand that to look at this solely from the viewpoint of people with learning disabilities' rights is to oversimplify an intensely complex subject. Ultimately the rights of people with learning disabilities will be enhanced, if their parents' concerns are acknowledged.

All the names in this book have been changed in order to respect the confidentiality of those concerned.

Acknowledgements

We are deeply indebted to the many parents, carers, people with learning disabilities and workers who have shared so much with us and helped us to understand something of their realities.

We are also very grateful to the 13 parents/carers whose generosity has allowed us to quote from what they have told us of their experiences. This breath of 'real life' greatly enhances what we have to say.

Many other people have encouraged and supported us in the preparation and writing of the book, to whom we are also grateful.

Finally our thanks go to Barnardos for seeing that sexuality is central to the lives of people with learning disabilities and for allowing sufficient space for the book to be written.

Introduction

This book is for parents and carers of people with learning disabilities. Its goal is to help parents feel more comfortable and confident when thinking about sex and sexuality in relation to their son or daughter who has a learning disability. Other people, such as residential staff and social workers, may also find it useful, but our main purpose is to look at the subject from the parents' and carers' point of view. Often, parents' views are not given the weight they deserve and this book tries to restore a balance.

For a number of years now, we have been working with people with learning disabilities and their parents and carers, as well as with workers from education, social services and the voluntary sector. The twin aims of our work are to help people with learning disabilities to:

- have a right to be sexual
- be better protected from sexual abuse.

From our experience we have come to believe that you, as parents, are crucial in ensuring such aims are supported and in a responsible fashion. You are likely to have a particular knowledge of your son or daughter's disability and a special understanding of what this means in their day-to-day life. So any discussion of sexuality must involve you. However, sexuality is a difficult subject; it probably is for most parents, let alone those who have a child with a learning disability. It can be a painful journey that may not have a clear end in view. We hope this book will help you to extend your thinking and enable you to cope with all the feelings that go with that.

Our experience in this field comes from our daily work. Many parents have talked to us about their experiences and views and these form a crucial part of the book. One of us is also a carer of a young adult with physical and learning disabilities. We work with parents of children and adults with learning disabilities, most of whom are the birth parents. However, we have also included views of parents who foster long-term and those who provide a shared care service on an ongoing basis. Their sons and daughters range widely in age and disability, from mild-moderate to severe and profound. Much of what we say can be applied generally across all ages and disabilities, although, where specific elements need to be taken into account, we have tried to do that.

Finally, we offer this book in a spirit of optimism. People with learning disabilities are achieving more in their lives than ever before and experiencing greater opportunities. The fact that there are considerable difficulties and challenges in making those become a reality is no reason for us to lose our nerve. But we must first make a Health Warning. While preparing this book, we spoke to a number of parents who told us the stories of their families' journeys through disability. We knew that for some this would open up a box of memories and experiences, which were sometimes joyful, but were often painful. We know that any parent of a person with learning disabilities will have had similarly harrowing experiences and memories, probably starting at the time of diagnosis (or when you realised there was something wrong, which may have been long before the medical profession did) and possibly continuing into the present. Some-how parents find a way to deal with these difficulties. Often the way this is done is by wrapping them up and burying them away deep inside, hidden from view. However, just as we knew that speaking to parents could evoke discomforting memories for them, so we know that reading this book may arouse equally distressing emotions for you. We do want you to read this book, as we believe it says very important things and will be of help to many parents. It is our hope that we will be able to give you useful insights and practical ideas to help you convert some of what for you could be painful experiences into a powerful energy that will sustain you as you move on in your journey.

1 Don't Mention the 'S' word

For most of us the subject of sexuality brings out a potent mixture of emotions, ranging from fear, confusion or embarrassment to something wonderfully strengthening and life enhancing. It all depends on many things, in particular, our experiences, past and present and the current situation in which we find ourselves. These days sex and sexuality are both a public and yet intensely personal part of life where, on the one hand, there can be strict codes about what's right and wrong, and yet, on the other, it seems that anything goes. Having a clear sense of what sexuality means for us as individuals, and being content with that, contributes to our enjoyment of happy and fulfilled lives. If the reality for most of us falls a little short of that ideal, then consider the situation for people with learning disabilities. For them sexuality is usually only mentioned as an 'issue', a 'problem' where a need to know is discouraged and basic rights (including the right to be safe) can be subtly denied. There are all sorts of reasons why this is so and we're not saying that anyone is to blame. What we have to do is own up to that, try to understand why it is so, and work out how to move forward.

WHAT DO WE MEAN BY 'SEX' AND 'SEXUALITY'?

We spend a lot of time discussing the terms 'sex' and 'sexuality' with parents and professionals, and know how important it is to agree on definitions.

'Sex' is commonly used to mean gender – whether you're male or female. It is also used to describe the physical act of sexual intercourse. On the other hand, 'sexuality' refers to the whole person – thoughts, feelings, beliefs, behaviours towards oneself and others as well as the body and how it works.

The following definition from Hilary Dixon neatly explains this:

> Sexuality is the way I experience myself as a woman (or man) and how I relate to others. It includes my self-esteem; the roles I am given or take on; the way I communicate with others; my relationships; my body – how it works and how I use it. It is much more than genitals and their reproductive function.

This definition works because it holds together the reality of what we have just described as sex and sexuality. It also applies to everyone – whether young or old, sexually active or inactive, celibate, heterosexual or homosexual, disabled or not disabled. It is deeply respectful and provides a good basis for how this whole subject can be discussed in relation to people with learning disabilities.

There's an important point to make here about what we call the 'biological imperative'. Sexual sensations and feelings are a physical and biological reality for just about everybody, regardless of intellectual capacity and physical ability. We can't pretend otherwise. Denying that is one reason why many people with learning disabilities have problems with their sexuality.

In an excellent book called *Shared Feelings*, the author Diane Maksym says that sex is inborn, an easily identified part of us, from the minute we arrive into the world. Sexuality, on the other hand, she says, is something we learn. For example, being born male or female is (largely) a fixed part of us, whilst our understanding about, and feelings of, masculinity and femininity are learned from other people as we grow and mature. By watching and listening to other people, we learn what to say, how to behave in various settings, and how different people are to be responded to. We learn about what behaviour is right for public places and what has to be kept private, whom we can touch in particular ways, and the right time and place for sexual activity. Through all this we're also learning about ourselves and what makes us tick, hopefully in ways that gradually build up a positive sense of ourselves and our own worth. Diane Maksym describes this as like learning a script in a play. We each have our own script, which is made up of two parts. The first consists of values and attitudes about sexuality we learn from many sources – our parents, religious teachings, the culture we are a part of, our friends, the media and so on. To some degree this is already written for us: we only have to learn it. The second part is what we write ourselves, as we apply our inherited guide and then decide what we believe, like, or wish to do in our own lives, as sexual beings.

How did you learn about sexuality? And, what script did you learn as you were growing up? The following exercise adapted from Diane Maksym's *Shared Feelings* might be a useful way for you to answer this. You could try to answer it on your own, or, better still, with your partner or a close friend. There are no right or wrong answers; the questions are there to get you thinking.

- What feelings do you remember having about being a boy or girl? Did your parents, and other adults, treat you differently from children of the other gender?
- What were your family rules or customs about nudity, privacy and touching?
- What memories do you have of exploring your own body? If your parents knew of it, what was their reaction?
- How did you learn about sex or the facts of life? How much from your parents, school and friends? Can you recall your feelings at the time? Was the information accurate?
- When did you first become aware that your parents had sex? What were your feelings at the time?
- What memories do you have about your body beginning to change from that of a child; your first period; wet dreams?
- What memories do you have of your first date, your first kiss and your feelings at the time?

You've probably found that most of your learning was simply a gradual process, although you may recall the times when something significant was heard or experienced for the first time. In our role as parents we are part of the process by which our children come to grips with sexuality and what that means for them. Whatever our beliefs about sex education (specifically information on the facts of life), we are, in the very way we bring up our children, shaping their sexuality. This is so whether we are aware of it or not. Children learn from their parents directly and by the example set them. They copy us, repeat what we say. Their self-worth is bound up in the way all this is done. Our children's main sexuality educators are ourselves. This is equally so if they have a learning disability, although how they absorb and take it in will not necessarily be the same as for other children.

WHAT DO CHILDREN LEARN ABOUT SEXUALITY?

What it means to be a girl or a boy

It is thought that by the age of two years, most children have a clear sense of being either a girl or a boy, and that there are differences between the two. In the years following we see children playing a variety of games in which this is explored – Mummies and Daddies, going to work and staying at home, dressing up. We confirm the separate gender identities in the clothes children wear, their hairstyles, the toys and games given to them, the way we talk to them. Certainly books and television programmes play their part too.

Being loved and valued

This is conveyed in a multitude of ways: by word, gesture, tone of voice, facial expression, body language. All these say whether the child is truly appreciated for her/himself, his/her uniqueness. It all adds up to a sense of self-esteem, which is a crucial part of human sexuality. If children grow up being made to feel unworthy, they do not have a good opinion of themselves and find it hard to develop trusting relationships.

Inquisitiveness about their own bodies

It is natural for children to explore their bodies. We see babies discovering their fingers and toes and gradually learning that they are separate beings to their parents. This natural exploration continues with discovering their genitals and the nice sensations that can come with touching them. At this point, a parent may try to stop or distract the child, fearing that such exploration might be seen as 'sexual' in an adult sense. Such curiosity is a perfectly normal part of children's growth, development and understanding of themselves. Children also engage in play that observes or even explores each other's bodies. We tend to read adult experiences and attitudes into this, although it may simply signify a way of adding to their growing store of knowledge.

Friendships

These are a vital component in healthy and fulfilling lives. Within friendships children can work on social skills, measure themselves in relation to their peers, find 'safe' places for sharing secrets, gain solidarity against the adult world. Around the age of nine, ten or 11, there may be early and tentative practice for later sexual relationships, with talk of having a boy or girlfriend. Boys will be interested in each other's penis size; girls will be sharing the waiting for 'starting' their first period.

Puberty and body changes
As well as physical changes, children develop sexual feelings and may indeed have sexual fantasies. It's a time of great self-absorption and worry about whether what's happening is normal. Most boys will be masturbating by puberty, so will some girls. It's a time when the wider definition of sexuality is now moving to its core, that is, the genitals: what they're for and how they work.

Preparing for life as an adult
They will be continuing to learn about adult roles and responsibilities, one obvious one, will be starting to have boy- and girlfriend relationships and sexual experimentation. If the young person has been prepared well enough for this stage, they will hopefully participate in safe enough ways. The adolescent years should ideally be free from inappropriate adult responsibilities, so that young people have space and opportunity to test out their attitudes and beliefs, taste new experiences, develop a wider range of relationships, and work out for themselves the sort of person they would like to be. During this stage, parents are beginning to 'let go', and learning themselves how to live with the possible – both positive and negative – consequences of that. By late adolescence, the majority of parents are probably looking forward to the time (now fast approaching) when their children will be 'off their hands'; although, in reality, it is rarely as easy as that. However, for parents of a child with learning disabilities, it is a time to realise afresh that the responsibility of close and supervisory parenting is not going to lessen after all.

2 Sexuality and learning disability

Sexuality has long been a taboo subject, and only in recent years has it begun to be discussed more openly. As the poet Philip Larkin commented wryly, 'sex wasn't invented until 1963'. Sexuality is so personal to us and so bound up in the life story of each one of us that it is impossible to treat it impersonally, as we can most other subjects. Our sexuality is fundamental to who we are as human beings. We can't separate ourselves from our sexuality, it is integral to us. In many ways our society appears to have gone from one extreme to the other. A generation ago sexuality was little talked about, at least not publicly, and was largely covert. Now, it seems, there are images of sexuality wherever we look, we are bombarded with it on television, in films, music, and advertising. Yet it can still be difficult for couples, even those who feel they know each other intimately, to talk about sexuality. It can be the most difficult subject to discuss candidly because none of us like to have our vulnerabilities and insecurities exposed.

Perhaps the problem is that we mistake sexuality for sex; that is, we narrow our thinking down just to sexual activity. By failing to look at sexuality (with its meaning broader than simply genital functioning), the whole subject becomes much more difficult to deal with. Embarrassment, lack of confidence, uncertainty are likely to be the dominant feelings.

With regard to people with learning disabilities and sexuality, many parents and professionals see only problems. This is understandable when the person concerned is behaving inappropriately. However, we must ask ourselves whether this inappropriate behaviour would have happened if sexuality had been considered right from the start?

> ### Jack
> *When Jack was 14 we were faced with a problem that meant we could no longer forget he was soon to be a man. A neighbour telephoned us in hysterics to tell us that she had looked out of her window and seen Jack 'waving his thingy' at her across the road. As a family we were mortified – it was bad enough being singled out in the village as having two disabled children, but now this! Our only contact with professionals was a paediatrician who, on the advice of a psychiatrist, prescribed a drug to dampen down Jack's sexual feelings. Nobody suggested that what he was doing was normal and what we needed was help to encourage him to masturbate only in privacy. Alarmingly, Jack reacted to the drug and suffered spasms of thoracic paralysis. Only the quick thinking of a casualty doctor averted a possible disaster.*
>
> *Sandra, mother of Jack aged 33 and Tim aged 24.*

This happened 20 years ago. How different might it be today?

Sexuality is inseparable from self-esteem, and, if our self-esteem is damaged in some way, then the likelihood is that this will affect our sexuality and our sexual behaviour. For example, people who feel a lack of self-esteem may become totally compliant – doing what others want of them – if this makes them feel valued and wanted. They may even become entangled in a violent relationship: fearful of their partner, yet unable to consider life without them. Others may go on to exploit other people, in a vain attempt to build up their own self-esteem; they may feel worthless, but believe that if they bully others, it might force people to respect them. One thing is clear, who we are as sexual people is very much dependent on what is going on in the rest of our lives. The two things are inextricably linked. If we fail to address our sexuality and understand it, then it can only have a negative effect on the rest of our lives.

It is only in the past 30 years or so that we, as a society, have begun to deal with the lives of people with learning disabilities in a fairer and just way. The history of society's attitude to learning disability before that is largely a shameful one, and reflects a lack of understanding and acceptance of people with learning disabilities as unique and valuable individuals. Why did this happen? Below, we explore a number of possible reasons.

Fear of the unknown

Unless people were given opportunities to get to know them personally, those with learning disabilities have been viewed by most as though they were aliens from another planet. For most people their first encounter with disability is when a child with a disability is born into their own family, or a member of their family becomes disabled. For people without such first-hand experience of disability it is unfamiliar territory. And, put simply, what we don't know about, we often fear.

Culture of rejection

Until recently, there was every reason for most people to know little about learning disability. Many people with learning disabilities were put away in places of incarceration, such as long-stay hospitals on distant moors, which pretended to provide asylum for vast numbers of people, while actually denying their individuality and basic human rights. Prior to the Industrial Revolution, some people with learning disabilities would have had a work role within the home or their immediate community. But as people moved from small rural communities into towns and worked in factories, people with learning disabilities had no place; they began to be seen as a burden. Those unable to keep up with fast-moving machine operations were condemned to the workhouse, or similar, along with others who were seen as either lazy or sinful. Until relatively recently, parents of children with learning disabilities were positively encouraged to place those children in care, usually in large hospitals, and told to 'forget' them, after which, contact was often quickly lost. The child then grew up into an adult with no family connections, cared for by a 'profession' based on institutional living. For most, their earlier history became lost for ever.

Tainted by association

Many people are afraid to be associated with people with learning disabilities because they feel they would be tainted or marked in some way. This is sad for people with learning disabilities because sometimes the rejection they experience is obvious and hurtful. You probably have examples in your own life where this has or is happening. It is also sad for non-disabled people who are unable to take the opportunity to widen their understanding of learning disability, thereby deepening their own humanity. This difficulty springs from a human need to be part of the group and its beliefs, and so be accepted; to think differently runs the additional risk of being rejected, which would be hard for most people. Insecurity runs very deep within humanity.

SEXUALITY AND CHILDREN WITH LEARNING DISABILITIES

Do children with learning disabilities learn about their sexuality in the same way as non-disabled children? The answer, in principle, is more yes than no, although the degree to which individual children really do develop such awareness depends on a number of factors:
- the nature and extent of their disability
- their opportunities for learning
- their life experiences and . . . most importantly . . .
- the attitudes of adults like yourselves who look after them.
    Let's look at this more closely.

You will know better than anyone the way in which your child learns about herself and the world around her. If she has brothers or sisters you probably, almost automatically, compare the pace of her learning with theirs. There might be some things she picks up really well but, overall, her learning is likely to be markedly slower. This will depend of course on the learning disability and its severity. It may take a child a long time to understand properly that boys are one thing, girls another, let alone why there is a difference. We worked with a group of young adults who had moderate to severe learning disabilities. Whilst they knew who was male and who was female and which gender they each belonged to, they knew little about the reasons for the difference, nor much about the different private body parts. It could be that no one had ever given them that information. It could also be that none of them had ever asked the sort of questions that children usually ask in order to satisfy their growing curiosity, or if they had, that no satisfactory answers had been given.

The way children with a learning disability come to understand aspects of sexuality – such as whether they are a boy or
girl – is completely individual to them and their circumstances. It
will largely depend on their ability and on the opportunities they
have to explore their own body, to develop and participate in
meaningful relationships, to experience puberty without fear or
confusion, and to know themselves to be loved and valued. It is
also unlikely to be straightforward. A number of reasons for this
are given below.

Learning is at a slower pace

It is also more complicated than that. Each child learns in their
own particular way and what works for one may not for another.
Repetition will be necessary, as well as breaking down information into small, maybe even minute components.

Segregation

There have been huge changes to the previous 'invisibility' of
people with learning disabilities. The principle of inclusion, a
greater integration within education, the development of community care and group homes, supported employment, ordinary
leisure and social opportunities: all these elements are part of a
right and just move that says people with disabilities are as
precious and valuable as we ourselves would like to be viewed.
Yet most still experience a degree of separation from mainstream
society. There are many consequences of this. For example,
children placed within special schools are cut off from the
casual, *ad hoc* way in which most children acquire information
on sex and the way bodies work. Children with learning disabilities who cannot, or do not, play with their non-disabled
peers are deprived of opportunities for ordinary play experiences
and group games in which learning can develop and uncertain-
ties and fantasies worked through. At a deeper level, even young
people with quite severe learning disabilities may sense that they
are 'apart' and feel this exclusion.

Lack of privacy

As most children grow up they learn to keep part of their lives a
secret from adults, especially if they sense there may be disap-
proval. This is a part of the natural process of children gradually
transferring wholehearted allegiance from their parents to their

peers and other adults, thereby widening their circle of influence. Children are then able to test out their parents' beliefs, attitudes and ways of going about life against those of other people. By contrast the life and ways of a child with learning disabilities often remain an open book to the parents. This may be a natural consequence of the disability and level of care and supervision required. For example, children requiring a high degree of personal care will not easily be able to develop a sense of their body being 'private' to them. This will be the case no matter how carefully and respectfully the care is given. The secret (and forbidden?) chance to talk 'bodies and bits' with other children and the 'I'll show you mine if you show me yours' challenge which non-disabled children engage in are hard or impossible for those with significant disabilities. Watching and protectiveness by adults may also reduce the opportunity for this sort of quite natural activity.

The need to wear nappies and incontinence pads
This does lessen the opportunity for exploring the body. Some parents we have talked to recognise this and leave their child in a safe place without such physical restrictions, so exploring can be done if the child wishes. In a group home for young adults with severe physical and learning disabilities, sensitively minded staff told us that they had bought Kylie sheets (bed linen that allows moisture to seep through to a lower layer, thus keeping the top layer, next to the skin, dry). One young man would be left on a Kylie sheet after a relaxing bath, in private, and without pads so that he could masturbate. The attitude of staff, which accepted this young man's right to a sexual life, made it possible for this to be carried out in privacy and with dignity.

Communication between parent and the child with learning disabilities
It is quite likely that your child takes her/his cue from you about whether being disabled is OK or not. Children soon pick up whether their parents are deeply sad or anxious, even when few words are said. When you are positive and hopeful, that too will communicate itself. Tone of voice, body posture, facial expressions, even silences, all 'speak' volumes. Whatever you say or do, your child is probably very good at tuning into this.

> *Looking through his tears he saw her as she bent low in order to look into his eyes. 'I never prayed for you to be born crippled,' she said. 'I wanted you to be full of life, able to run and jump and talk just like Yvonne. But you are you, you are Joseph not Yvonne . . . Listen here Joseph . . . you are loved by me and Dad. We love you just as you are.' He was only three years in age but he was now fanning the only spark he saw, his being alive and more immediate, his being wanted just as he was.*
>
> Christopher Nolan

Attitudes of parents and other carers

These are picked up by children. Whatever parents think about sexuality and sexual matters will be heard and absorbed by their children, even if not properly understood. 'That's dirty', 'you're too young', 'take that hand away I tell you' delivered in a horrified or condemnatory tone of voice with accompanying facial expressions, gossipy opinions about other people's lives can all send unhelpful messages to children that are likely to confuse them. Parents may have another problem here, in that behaviour appropriate to a young age is not necessarily appropriate at an older one. For example, it's generally OK for a three-year-old to strip off on the beach, but definitely not appropriate at 33, or 23 or even 13. We've been told by parents with an autistic child that behaviour learned and exhibited at a young age is likely to be there for life. In a sense, then, those parents have to think 'adult' even when their child is very young. Over the years we have spent a lot of time in a special school for children with severe learning disabilities aged three to 19. Until a change of headship, many of the children and young people were allowed to greet visitors, known and unknown, in whatever way they chose. Much of this involved hugging – completely inappropriate for the child and potentially unsafe. The attitude of most staff was that there was nothing wrong. A new broom swept all clean. *All* children and young people are taught and supported in socially appropriate greetings, so where there was once hugging, there is now handshaking, appropriate physical distance being kept and eye contact achieved. How much better for the children and young people to be encouraged and supported in behaving just like everyone else. However, this is not necessarily so easy as it sounds. C. aged 15, very attractive and with a severe learning disability, *still* runs up to strange men in the local supermarket and tries to claim their attention by word and action. A programme is being worked out with the aim of making her behaviour more appropriate and therefore safer.

Letting go
This continues the point made above. Parents are making judgements all the time about what is safe for their children to do and constantly reassessing that as the child gets older and gains in experience and confidence. Where the child has a learning disability this is more complicated. Awareness of risk and the dependence of the child usually result in close protection. Whilst this may reassure the parent, the child may be disadvantaged. Thinking of how all children grow and mature, opportunities to assess and manage risk are needed – walking to school, playing outdoors, going to the local shop, into town with their friends, first time alone in the house – all these are a part of normal development. For good and understandable reasons, it is hard for parents to let their children who have learning disabilities experience risk in case they are harmed as a result. For the child, being 'wrapped up' adds to a sense of being different, apart from other people. This may well keep self-esteem low.

Acquiescence
One dictionary definition says this means 'to consent quietly without protest, but also without enthusiasm'. You may say that your child is not one who easily complies with what you or any other (trusted) adults require! However, it does seem to be a characteristic of learning disability that individuals wish to please, say what they think the other person wants to hear: saying 'yes' when really meaning 'no', appearing to give consent when in fact it is absent, or appearing to understand when in fact she/he does not. We talk much more about this in Chapter 6.

Myths and stereotypes
There are two main beliefs about people with learning disabilities and sexuality, which completely contradict each other. The first is that people with learning disabilities are sex-mad and

always 'at it'. The second is that they are sexless and have no sexual feelings whatsoever. Clearly both views are wrong and give a completely misleading impression of learning disability. It's also worth saying that if any person who has a learning disability does appear to behave in a way that confirms either statement, it is likely to be because of the attitudes of others or experiences in their lives that have led them to that situation; not because they have a learning disability. Faced with this, people with learning disabilities will nearly always find it hard to feel good about their sexuality and able to take in the learning that is needed. These myths should be seen for what they are – unhelpful and inaccurate.

A social attitude

Whilst our society is making some progress in valuing people with learning disabilities as precious individuals in their own right, the idea that they might reproduce themselves, that is, become parents (possibly having a child who also has learning disabilities) raises concern. For the parent of a son or daughter with learning disabilities, that concern or fear might be about having to care for the baby because their son or daughter possibly cannot. Such beliefs may be absorbed or in some way heard by the person with learning disabilities. There is a lot of evidence describing how many young women with learning disabilities have been sterilised without their full knowledge and consent, or had their babies taken away, and been at the receiving end of professional views that they cannot be parents or raise children.

Yet through all this, young people with learning disabilities are learning about sex and sexuality. Given that reality, it's really important that we take some control of the situation and try to make sure that what they do learn is right for them – according to age and ability. In Chapter 8 we look at sexuality work/sex education and how parents can best be involved.

Many parents find it really difficult to think about sexuality in respect of their child, particularly so if they have a child who is disabled. To be fair, parents already have an enormous amount on their plates and coping with that on a day-to-day basis can be hard enough. Where the thought does occur, especially whilst the child is still young, the natural instinct is probably to put it right at the back of the mind and lock it away. But the door which is locked will open, like it or not, when puberty arrives, bodies develop and hormones surge. We can't deny that reality or even wish it away; much better to face the facts and make a plan that responds appropriately to the needs of that young person.

3 The grieving process: denial and acceptance

Sexuality when coupled with disability is a complex subject, which highlights our own need to accept ourselves as sometimes weak and insecure. That is, after all, what makes us human. Parenthood is particularly prone to expose these insecurities. As the old joke has it, the one thing that doesn't come with a baby is an instruction manual. The experience of parenthood is complicated further when the child is learning disabled. In order successfully to negotiate bringing up a child who is learning disabled and who is not 'perfect' in the eyes of the world, it is necessary to grieve for the 'lost child'; in other words, the child you were expecting but did not have. This is not meant to be disrespectful to any learning disabled person, it is merely the process by which parents come to terms with their reality, and enables some to accept and others to go further and celebrate their child.

GRIEVING – THE DIAGNOSIS

The period immediately following diagnosis can play a crucial role in the grieving process. If the diagnosis is handled badly (and our conversations with many parents suggests that, sadly, this is often the case), then the grieving process can be blocked, or flawed from the start. How the disclosure is done and the information about the disability given are crucial to how well parents are able to deal with it intellectually and emotionally.

Stuart
Stuart was born in some distress because the cord was round his neck. I caught a brief glimpse of him before he

went to the Special Care Baby Unit and I said, 'He's a Mongol baby'. There were a number of medical people around, none of whom responded at the time. After I had slept, the paediatrician came to see me and explained in a balanced way that Stuart could be Down's, although one of the signs was absent in him. A blood test was needed, which would take a few days to come through. I was gutted at the news and cried and cried. An older midwife on duty at the time told me to walk away because she said he'll be a burden. In contrast, a young junior doctor visited me several times while I was in hospital, usually at the end of a long shift, which was very late evening. He told me about his brother who had Down's and had led and was leading a purposeful and good life. His attitude was entirely positive. I remember his care and his words with great appreciation, and though I cried a great deal with him, his visits helped me to cope with the emotions and face the future in a positive frame of mind. When the results of the blood tests were through, the paediatrician visited myself and my husband at home to give us the results and to answer all our questions. Also, he was able to put us in touch with another parent who had a son with Down's and lived in the area. Our grieving was done at this time for the non-disabled child that we didn't have.

Judith, mother of Stuart, aged 13

The negative comments Judith received about Stuart from the midwife were fortunately replaced by the positive ones given by the junior hospital doctor and the paediatrician. The time and care given by both these people also made a huge difference to the way she was able to hear and deal with the facts. Judith commented: 'it's very hard for the professionals to get it right because, no matter what they say, it won't be right for everybody'. This makes it really important that professionals are sensitive to the situation and try to assess what seems to be the 'right way' at that time.

Differences occur when it is the parent who first senses things 'aren't right' and it is the professionals who are not ready to listen. Then parents are coping with their feelings of uncertainty and anxiety without anything concrete or confirmed to pin them to. This is especially difficult if the professionals are reluctant to break the news.

> *I suspected something was wrong after about four weeks. Jack seemed to lack the reflexes you expect in a young baby. But even a relative who was a district nurse said, 'Don't be silly, he's fine'. When the health visitors did come to assess him some time later, my husband took him out before the assessment was finished. Nobody could bear to accept the reality of a second disabled child in the family.*
> *Sandra, mother of Jack aged 33 and Tim aged 24.*

Sandra goes on:

> *When Tim was six months old I saw the specialist who said he was not reaching his milestones, and I lied. I told him that he was smiling when in fact he was not. I wanted him to have a physical disability, thinking, that with physiotherapy, we could put things right. But to admit that he wasn't smiling would have been admitting that he was possibly a child with learning disabilities and that was too much to bear.*

Professionals are not immune to these feelings; they can also find it all 'too much to bear'. Sandra gives this example:

> *The paediatrician told me he was a month behind in his development. When I saw Tim's notes (which the doctor left on the table) it said he was two months behind! I suppose they are just human beings and they cannot cope with people's suffering any more than anyone else can.*

Mother of Terry, aged 20, Ruth's experience was also of being the first to spot things were not well: 'Terry was six months old when I noticed the problem.' Initially she was assured that Terry could 'catch up' but, finally, when Terry was 15 months old, Ruth was 'very brutally told' by her GP that, 'Terry is brain damaged'. Ruth also makes a distinction between a child born with an obvious disability, such as Down's Syndrome, and situations such as hers where the reality becomes apparent some time later: 'when the disability is not immediately obvious, and thus able to be diagnosed, you suddenly lose the "perfect" child you thought you had'.

THE PROCESS OF GRIEVING

'It is an ongoing process – not an event that begins and ends.'

Theresa, mother of Max, aged 13

We've talked about the need for parents to face their deepest feelings about their child's disability as soon as they can. This doesn't mean that distressing times are past: far from it. Lizzie, mother of Kate aged eight, experienced the diagnosis of Down's Syndrome being given in a positive way and has since then self-consciously sought to maintain a sense of optimism about Kate's life. However, since Kate's birth, Lizzie has 'highs and lows' of feelings, according to the state of Kate's achievements, problems, behaviours, learning, and not learning. For example, when Kate began to crawl, Lizzie was 'ecstatic' and immediately ran to tell a neighbour. Yet the constant reminders of Kate's slow level of development continue to cause her deep anguish.

As anyone who has ever lost a loved one knows, grieving takes time. If the time is not there in those early days, then the process will be put on hold. Rather than going away, it remains buried, resurfacing, unbidden, maybe many times in the months and years that follow. And it will continue to resurface until it gets the attention it needs. Shock, denial, anger, regret, loss and acceptance are all part of that grieving process. These and other emotions do not register only at the time of diagnosis, they are felt to some degree throughout the child's life. But the extent to which they are experienced and made sense of in those early days and months does contribute to their longer-term impact, and whether that is lighter or heavier. Working through this grief is essentially about accepting the reality of the disability with a good heart.

Growing up with Disability argues that therapies such as the Doman Delacato method, so popular in the 1970s, and Conductive Education in the 1980s, gives a child: 'a very clear message that there is something about them that nobody likes'. For some parents, the strong desire to pursue approaches like this may well be a response to what they see is a shortcoming in the services offered to them; but it could also be that the process of grieving, acceptance and coming to terms with the situation, is not complete. The idea that, with alternative theories, or hard work and dedication, you can make your child normal, is common to many parents. This is not to say that these methods don't have value, or that by accepting the situation we are advocating complete defeat. (And by using terms such as 'acceptance' and 'coming to terms with' we do not mean a passive response that is low on energy and action, of 'giving in', and relinquishing all hope of any change.) What we have in mind is a more dynamic response where the facts of the disability are faced and understood both with the head and the heart.

Once parents can do that they are free to take appropriate and informed action, confident in sharing that reality with others – relatives, friends, neighbours and the myriad professionals who will become a regular part of their lives. Then the very best within the situation and the individuals involved can be brought out. Many parents have used this creative energy to challenge service providers, become more expert in their child's condition than most of the professionals they encounter, and befriend other parents in similar positions.

It is true to say that with the birth of a child who has learning disabilities lives are changed for ever. This is so for the parents, other children in the family and, usually to a lesser extent, for the extended family. There is a line in *The Prophet* by Kahlil Gibran where he speaks of the suffering part of loving. He talks about people who have not experienced the deep cost of loving and whose lives are therefore only half lived.

> *But if in your fear you would seek only love's*
> *peace and love's pleasure,*
> *Then it is better for you that you cover your nakedness and*
> *pass out of love's*
> *Threshing floor,*
> *Into the seasonless world where you shall laugh, but not all*
> *of your laughter,*
> *And weep, but not all of your tears.*
>
> *From Kahlil Gibran, The Prophet*

Whilst many parents of a disabled child wouldn't necessarily have chosen what happened to them, they do feel their life has been enriched, and their horizons broadened far more as a consequence.

When asked if he minded caring for his cousin, who had learning disabilities, George replied: 'No, it's just a bloody pain sometimes.'

MOVING FORWARD

Having the opportunity to express the sadness and the grief over not having the child expected can help parents to move forward. This is not to say that parents can't do so without being given this time; many have moved forward without needing to talk to someone about their feelings. It's just that, without this opportunity, either together or separately with someone else, couples can find themselves in difficulty. Their channels of communication with each other may close down, relationships can become brittle and it may take much longer to re-establish a point of equilibrium or balance in their lives. It can lead to stress and depression, which may take years to overcome. Having a sympathetic and trusted person, who can make the difference between recovering and remaining stuck in despair, is crucial. It is often the case, however, that the partner in the relationship is not that person. Who does provide the listening ear will be different according to each individual need. One parent (a mother) told us, 'perhaps fathers and mothers need different things in terms of support. Men are expected to be strong, to carry on. Maybe they need support independent of their wives' (Sandra).

GRIEVING AND SEXUALITY

When we interviewed parents, some said that at first they found this question of grieving an interesting one, but didn't really see how it related to a book on learning disability and sexuality. Our view is that families who are unable to grieve can become 'stuck': they cannot move on in their lives or their relationships, and sometimes this feeling can hang around for years. It can actually end up blocking people's personal growth for the rest of their lives. We feel it is a fundamental issue. If parents haven't been allowed, or are unable for a variety of reasons, to deal with early feelings of grief and loss, then acceptance of their child as she/he is, will be stunted, blocking their path to maturity.

'Max changed our lives for ever. Our journey became a different one. As the main carer, it was different for me, I learned to accept disability, to "love" it. My husband never did that, he said that I thought more about the support group than I did him.'

Theresa

Through speaking to people we have found that, where grief has not been entered into, relationships have suffered profoundly, sometimes irreparably.

IMPLICATIONS OF NOT GRIEVING

Perhaps most crucially, the impact is felt in terms of the parents' relationship. Sometimes when the grieving hasn't happened, and all feelings are in the emotional freezer, parents stop communicating with each other. They get on with the day to day, surviving until 'things gets better', putting off the difficult discussions and decisions until another day, when they expect to feel more able to cope. The trouble is that that day may never come. It's not just verbal communication that may suffer. Couples also communicate through their sexual relationship. If communication breaks down in their sexual relationship, this can lead to frustration, unhappiness, isolation, a loss of closeness and trust and, possibly, the ultimate breakdown of the relationship.

Meanwhile the child may become the focus for their staying together.

For parents of a child with a severe or profound learning disability, it can seem a terrible treachery to 'own up' to the dreams and wishes for the child whom you have wanted and expected; dreams in which the child would have grown up, met a partner, had a career and produced grandchildren. Yet if the grieving over this loss has taken place, and there has been a genuine acceptance of the child's disability, then parents are far more likely to be able to deal effectively and confidently with the sexuality issues as they arise for their learning disabled child. If parents are still blocked in their grieving process and denying the reality, then there is a chance that they may deny their child's sexuality as well.

The physical caring for a baby or young child with a severe disability and the emotional worry that goes with that can be absolutely exhausting. If parents are not 'together' in their situation, accepting it and working out how to live productively with it, then family life is diminished. Parents may disagree between themselves on how their child is to be cared for and reared: over-responding to crying bouts and, later, on issues such as discipline. There may be disagreement over how siblings are to be supported and involved, what services will be sought and how to negotiate with them. One parent, more likely the mother, may come to the point where she feels that only she really knows the child and her/his needs, which runs the risk of belittling and excluding the other partner's insights.

CONCLUSION

'There is a need both to grieve for the child they did not have and to come to love and accept the child they do have.'

Eileen Gascoigne

If, together, parents can work through their grief and sadness they may find that ultimately they are able to see their son or daughter as a sexual being. So the more parents are able to come to terms with the disability of child, the better able they are to welcome and promote the abilities and potential of that person. This is true in the case of sexuality no less than in the area of, for example, swimming or dance or anything else that their child may get involved with.

Those who have gone through the grieving process are more likely to be the ones able to look at the matter in a way that is healthiest for their son or daughter. Judith and her husband have been able to encourage Stuart to grow up in just the same way as his three siblings. Judith was aware from early on that Stuart had to be taught self-awareness: 'Nakedness has not been a problem in the family, so there has always been a relaxed and accepting attitude towards bodies and their functioning.' To reach such a level of understanding and coping is easier said than done, for the hopes and concerns of parents who have a child with a learning disability will always be at the forefront of their thoughts and actions. The next chapter looks more closely at the hopes and concerns of parents and how these can be a positive force in helping young people with learning disabilities lead safer and more fulfilled lives.

4 Parents' hopes and concerns

As parents, our hearts and minds are full of hopes and concerns for our children. The nature of these, however, changes as our children develop the ability to take more and more responsibility for themselves. When our children are little, our hopes and fears are often simple and short term: when will they begin to walk and talk?; is that a chest infection starting? As our children get older and wiser, these hopes and fears become much more expansive: what will he or she do for a career?; will they settle down with someone? We never stop being concerned about them, as those with grown-up children can testify. How often have we heard parenthood described in words similar to these: 'The first 18 years are terrible, you just worry about everything, desperately wanting to do whatever you can to make your child safe and happy. But once they get to 18, well, then it just gets worse.'

What a parent of a child with learning disabilities hopes for may well be outweighed by what they fear. This imbalance happens to parents of non-disabled children too, but usually only appears during a bad patch, when the child suffers an illness, is struggling at school, or has problems with their relationships. When that bad patch is put behind them, these fears subside and are replaced by hopes for the future once more; the child gets better, their school performance picks up, they resolve the problems in their relationships. For parents of a child with learning disabilities, fears tend to be something that are part of each and every day. This is not to suggest that having a disabled child is all problems and little joy – far from it – but most, if not all, parents and carers of a disabled child will confirm the extent to which their lives have been for ever changed by the reality of the disability.

The effect of disability upon family life, family relationships, energy levels, and self-confidence depends on a wide variety of factors. These are just a few, some of which we've already mentioned. You can probably add some more of your own:

- The nature and extent of the disability
- How the knowledge of it was first given by doctors
- What support is (or is not) available
- The attitudes and responses of other people such as relations and neighbours
- The almost unremitting battle for the most basic resources and services
- The relationship between the parents themselves.

What these things mean for individual families will not necessarily be the same. We are all different as people and bring our own unique strengths and weaknesses to our circumstances. This means we cope with them in our own special and distinctive ways. But all families, and the individuals within them, are never the same once disability becomes a part of their daily life. That is the reality.

In our work with parents and carers (as well as through our own personal experiences as parents and carers), we are well aware of how anxious, fearful, tired and insecure parents feel at times. Add the subject of sex and sexuality to the already hectic day-to-day routines and life can seem particularly difficult. Having said that, many parents do feel very positive about their circumstances, including issues around their child's sexuality – it is a mistake for parents (as with all people) to be thought of as being the same.

Read the following two statements from parents and see which seems the closest to your own view of your child's sexuality.

First Parent:
What if professionals tell me that my child has rights, including sexual rights, when they don't know what it's like for me or have any understanding of what it would really mean for me and my child?

Second Parent:
I am desperate for my child to have some sex education work done, but no one is willing to help or advise me.

There seems to be a big difference of opinion here. The first parent fears that their child will become even more vulnerable through the intervention of professionals, while the second parent believes that sexuality work will help reduce or manage the child's vulnerability but doesn't know where to go for help. But maybe these opinions are two sides of the same argument? You may well find you agree with both statements.

Now consider the following case studies. Do any of these remind you of your own situation?

Sally

Mrs S. is worried about her daughter, Sally, who is aged 15. Since puberty, Sally has been showing an increasing interest in men. With a severe learning disability (and minimal knowledge of sexuality issues) she has little understanding of danger. She tries to sit on any man's lap and, on occasions, has been known to start taking her clothes off.

Ravi

Ravi is aged 12 and has Down's Syndrome. He attends a local mainstream school. Always chatty and friendly, he has recently begun behaving in sexual ways with teachers and girls in his class, usually by touching breasts and the groin area. His parents are desperately looking for some form of help.

Maisie

Mrs B's 17-year-old daughter Maisie has cerebral palsy. She is physically and learning disabled. Maisie is determined to go to a residential college when she leaves school. Her mother asks the very reasonable question: 'How can I make sure she will be safe there when I am 100 miles away?'

Sara

Mr & Mrs T. are sure their 35-year-old daughter Sara has no interest whatsoever in sex. They don't discuss it at home and make sure she only watches TV programmes they think suitable. Despite this, when at the day centre, she refers to a man there as 'my boyfriend'.

Mark

Fifteen-year-old Mark has autism. He spends one week a month in a social services residential establishment. Staff have recently noticed that he is getting erections and trying to masturbate through his clothing. They are unsure about what to do, including whether to broach the subject with his father.

Where to start with any of these situations? The first reaction (of both parents and professionals) would probably be one of panic, of not knowing how to begin, worrying about jumping in at the wrong place and making matters even worse. What would you do? Who would you talk to about the problem? Would you know where to get help? Well, let us now look at how we could begin to tackle hopes and fears in a positive way.

The whole subject of sex and sexuality is so personal and sensitive, that in our workshops with parents we are careful to start at a point where they feel comfortable. For example, if someone is worried about what will happen to their five-year-old son when he reaches puberty, there's no point beginning with a session on contraception. We also need to take full account of parents' opinions and circumstances. We make no judgements, we simply try to create a friendly and supportive setting in which people feel safe enough to share their thoughts. This means parents are encouraged to say what they feel, not what they think the professionals want or expect to hear.

HOPES AND FEARS

In our workshops, one of the early exercises we undertake is called 'Hopes and Fears': In twos and threes, parents are invited to share their feelings about their child as a sexual person. These are then shared with the whole group, anonymously if that's what is preferred. A list of what many of these parents have said is given below. Perhaps unsurprisingly, parents from different groups usually come up with similar points.

Hopes
My daughter or son will
• be fully protected from abuse
• have a voice and be heard

- realise their dreams and be fulfilled
- regain the self-esteem experienced in earlier childhood years
- be accepted within the community when an adult as they are as a child
- form friendships and relationships of their own
- have a close personal friend to relate to
- be involved with professionals who can recognise their strengths
- be involved with professionals who have received the necessary and appropriate training
- be involved with professionals who listen to what parents have to say
- be better able to understand about sex and sexuality so that they can make reasonable decisions about their relationships (saying 'no' as well as 'yes').

Fears
About my son or daughter's
- vulnerability to abuse and harm
- puberty
- naïveté
- inability to indicate if she or he is being abused
- chronological age versus his/her emotional maturity
- inability to transfer learning from one situation to another
- lack of assertiveness, which might allow others to take advantage of her/him
- lack of understanding or ability to recognise potential danger
- inability to give informed consent
- tendency of living in a world of fantasy which he/she believes to be real
- future – 'what happens when I'm not here any more?'
- being seen as an adult even though he/she has the emotional maturity of someone much younger.

And other fears
- the danger of pregnancy
- that the family will not have the physical, mental or emotional stamina to cope with anything else
- that professionals may not have the answers
- that professionals will not listen or take on board their son/ daughter's vulnerability.

Many of these hopes are simply the reverse of some of the fears. For example, concern about vulnerability to abuse is linked to the hope that their child will be protected. As you'd expect, vulnerability and protection from abuse are enduring themes for all parents. The other hopes and fears tend to vary from one situation to another.

What are your feelings as you read the above lists? You may already be feeling positive and optimistic about your son or daughter's life, or perhaps the fears ring too many bells for you? Try thinking about your child's sexuality. What are your hopes and aspirations, your fears and concerns? Jot down your own lists and maybe share them with someone you trust.

If anxiety and uncertainty are uppermost in your mind, then it is even more important that you look at this issue sooner rather than later. Ideally, you should share your feelings with someone who can help you work through them – a partner, a friend, a fellow parent, or a trusted professional. If that person does not yet exist for you, don't despair. You have taken the first step towards acknowledging your feelings and the reality behind them. Facing them now gives you an opportunity to work out what needs to be done. There is a saying that 'there's nothing to fear but fear itself', so facing the fear of your child's future is a way of reducing anxiety, which allows you space to seek a solution. At the end of this book we've made some practical suggestions for what you might do in this and other circumstances.

'NOW I UNDERSTAND'

Two years ago we were involved with a group of parents from a local branch of the Down's Syndrome Association. Together we organised a conference for other parents on sex and sexuality in relation to young people with learning disabilities. Lizzie, mother of Kate aged eight, was involved in the planning. During that early stage she was clear that none of the content would relate to her as Kate was 'too young' but she was interested in the subject for future reference. After the event she said she was amazed at how wrong this view had been! She now understood that she should have been thinking about her daughter's sexuality from the moment she was born.

We believe that if parents are able to do this, to anticipate the time when their still young children are grown up, then several things will happen. First, they will be prepared, having a level of knowledge and understanding about their child that will make a huge difference to how they will feel and act when puberty does start. Secondly, they can start sexuality work proper with their child as soon as possible, which in reality is from when their lives begin. (We say more about this in Chapter 8). The difference this will make to their son or daughter is enormous. They too will be prepared for the reality of puberty and growing up, and will benefit from having a good level of self-esteem. They will also know that they have the support of someone close to them in this sensitive area, who understands what is happening to them. Thirdly, an important additional gain is that the child will be better protected from abuse and exploitation.

There are many good reasons why parents find it hard to think about their child as an adult and therefore a sexual being. Sometimes the sheer day-to-day slog soaks up all the available physical and mental energy. Thinking ahead means planning only as far as the next meal. As parents, we all find it difficult to think of the word 'sex' in relation to our young children, yet the time will inevitably come when we have to. This is easier to do if we remember the definition of the word sexuality given at the beginning of this book. Using that definition, it's correct to say that our children are sexual beings from the moment they are born, possibly even before that. To have a gender, as a boy or a girl in the womb, has already ensured that their sexuality will have a profound effect on their lives, whatever their level of ability and whether disabled or not.

But it's not just the very young who don't seem to fit comfortably into society's image of sexuality. Older and even middle-aged people are often seen as non-sexual. (Think of the discomfort we all felt when we first realised that our parents had sex in order to create us.) What does this mean for disabled older people? There is definitely a problem in society about people with physical or learning disabilities being sexually active and certainly about the idea of them becoming parents. These beliefs cannot help but influence our own thinking. For some parents who have a child with learning disabilities, it takes real courage and imagination to view their son or daughter as having the potential for a sexual relationship. There are some for whom this never will be possible because of the severity of the learning disability. That person can still be sexually active, such as by masturbation, but it can be hard for unprepared parents to consider that.

INFLUENCES AND PRESSURES

As parents of disabled children your hopes and fears are going to be formed by a variety of influences and pressures. These will include the following:

Society's attitudes towards people with learning disabilities
These attitudes are often confused, ambivalent, prejudiced, patronising and demeaning. Undoubtedly you will have experienced this for yourselves. We have had many examples given to us by parents – unsympathetic looks from fellow shoppers in the supermarket and even the occasional and incredibly cruel comment that the child 'should be locked up'.

The child's individual characteristics and personal resources
This is to do with their temperament, emotional well-being, personal history, self-awareness, knowledge and social skills. Severe deficits or problems in these areas will affect the child's ability to function effectively with the added layers of pressure that 'being disabled' can bring. This will inevitably influence whether, as their parent, your hopes outweigh your fears, or vice versa. On the other hand, some of the parents we have spoken to describe very positive characteristics in their children:

> *Terry can be very assertive when she wants to be. She knows her own mind. She can be very vocal.*
>
> *Ruth*

> *She has inner strength.*
>
> *Kim, mother of Tina aged 21*

> *Bill is caring and sensitive. He has standards. He has the capacity for understanding feelings.*
>
> *Jenny, mother of Bill, aged 20*

The reality of the learning disability

The learning disability may be diagnosed by medical professionals, and then assessed at various intervals by all sorts of other
professionals, but usually the people who know best what
an individual's learning disability really involves are her/his
parents. Only they fully understand the day by day experience of
the disability. Parents' fears are therefore especially real and
relevant, and are necessarily not just a case of being over-
protective or unrealistic, which is how some professionals consider them to be.

Accepting the reality

Parents wonder what might have been, had the child not been
disabled. This is made more apparent as the gap between the
child and his or her peers increases and milestones are missed or
reached later. Parents need to understand these feelings and not
to feel guilty about having them. By accepting them they can
learn to let them go and come to accept the reality of their
situation. And the reality is that normal expectations may not be
met, their child probably won't bear them grandchildren, their
child will always be more vulnerable than non-disabled children,
and their lives as carers will be very different to those of friends
with non-disabled children. Again the extent to which this
happens will be one of the key factors in the balance between
hopes and fears.

PROFESSIONALS' RESPONSES

Having encouraged parents to voice and share their hopes and
fears, we don't pretend that there are any easy answers; indeed, it
would be irresponsible to do so. Our aim is to acknowledge
them, to say to parents 'we accept the reality of your experiences, both good and bad'. This is something professionals
traditionally are not very good at. Professionals are trained to act,
to do something, to work towards solving problems, and above
all to instigate change. Acknowledging that there may not be a
clear way forward is hard for them. Parents may sense that the
doctor, social worker, nurse, cannot bear to hear the truths that
they (the parent) are describing. Sometimes, the workers will not
see protection in the way that parents do. It can be easy
for workers simply to judge parents as being over-protective,

without understanding why they appear to be so. For example, some people with learning disabilities seem very capable, but in fact have great gaps in their understanding and/or emotional maturity. Parents have daily experience and an intuitive grasp of that.

Professionals of all hues must be prepared to listen to the voice, heart and mind of what parents have to say. In situations where honest and open communication cannot or does not take place, the value of any support given is greatly diminished. In sharing their hopes and concerns with others, parents need to know that they are being heard and supported. Above all they need to know they are believed by professionals. They want to know that if there is to be a constructive way forward, the professional will fully include them in finding it. Equally, professionals must not be afraid to hear and deal with parents' sadness, pain, fear and hostility. It is difficult, but not impossible, to strike the right balance of meeting the basic human rights of someone with learning disabilities as a sexual person while also placing their right to be protected from abuse as a priority.

There is much yet to be done in developing a more constructive understanding between parents and professionals, and we believe that it is primarily the responsibility of professionals and agencies to make that happen.

At a recent workshop with parents, when the fear of vulnerability was being discussed, one parent challenged the professionals present by asking: 'How can I be sure that my daughter will be safe in your service?' We workers instinctively felt defensive. But the question was a crucial one, and it was important not to devalue it by false reassurance; after all, there's been plenty of evidence in recent years that vulnerable people are not always safe in our services (see Chapter 7). Acknowledging the parents' concerns and the reality of risks in even the best service provision helps to build trust. We were able, with the parents in the group, to develop a dialogue about what should be done, and who should be responsible for what, in order to reduce risks further.

5 'Them' and 'us'

This chapter is a tough one because it seeks to go to the heart of the question, namely: who knows best in the life of the learning disabled person? It is really about power and the balance of power – who holds it, is that fair, is it used responsibly? All of us are subject to various degrees of powerful influences which shape and determine our lives; that's part of a structured and organised society. However, some people are seriously disadvantaged by virtue of who they are, what they cannot do, the lifestyle they lead, the beliefs they hold . . . and many other reasons. These people tend to be on the margins of community life and are variously misunderstood, feared, patronised or pitied. This is certainly the case for many people with learning disabilities. By contrast, to have power is to be seen as strong and in a highly desirable position. Power comes in many forms – through knowing particular things (that most others do not), having intellectual skills or economic success, social status or a socially valued job or profession. On the whole, these things are not usually a part of the life of a person with learning disabilities.

People with learning disabilities are among the powerless in our society, and their parents, too, can be put in powerless positions, even if in other areas of their lives they experience success. In this chapter we're thinking of the relationships between professionals and parents, where there is definitely a degree of power difference. It is professionals who tend to have the power. As well as the respect that usually accompanies the professional role, professionals have the weight of important departments and organisations behind them. They have specialist knowledge and training, and often represent powerful people who make policy and hold large budgets. It is worth saying, though, that individual professionals may experience power-lessness at times, but are unlikely to feel the same sense of aloneness as a parent seeking more information or a better service for their child.

Parents are likely to feel themselves the junior partner in relationships with professionals, perhaps resulting in a need to 'keep in their good books' in order to receive the services they require. Even defining what is needed can be viewed differently by the parent and the professional. As well as the power that goes with the professional role, be it doctor, physiotherapist, teacher, social worker or social services manager, professionals have the added advantage of strength in numbers, knowing themselves to be part of a wider service-providing team. This 'array' of professionals may seem intimidating to parents, espe-cially a parent wanting to question or challenge what is being said or decided upon. An individual professional is not immune either – it is a particularly brave or determined individual to go against the beliefs or opinions of colleagues in support of a parent.

NOT ALL PROFESSIONALS HOLD POWERFUL POSITIONS

There is definitely a pecking order of most important and least important in status of workers within health, social services and education etc. The relevance of this for parent/professional relationships is that when parents are likely to be at their most vulnerable (around the time of diagnosis and sorting out what-ever therapy or treatment is required) that is when they are facing the most powerful of professionals – doctors and senior medical staff. As time passes parents relate to other profession-als, teachers and social workers, where the power differential, whilst still much in evidence, has narrowed.

By the time the person with learning disabilities has grown up, and especially if they attend a day centre, the power balance has altered yet again. Day centre staff tend to be amongst the lower paid within social services departments and feel themselves towards the bottom of the professional hierarchy. This may well result in low self-esteem and lack of confidence, which may have an impact on the quality of service provided. This is in spite of the great responsibilities such staff carry, the expectations placed on them to carry out departmental policies (which may seem to be forever changing), and a firm desire to do a good job.

PARENTS GAINING STRENGTH

By the time their daughter or son is using adult services, parents will be long accustomed to their role and many will have gained enormous confidence in negotiating and communicating with professionals. This personal growth and development of confidence and self-belief are very marked in a significant number of parents. These are people who, in other circumstances, might have been content to be in the background and not push themselves forward; accepting what is there. Having a disabled child changes them as people as well as their lives. The need to fight – for information, respect, services, a fair deal for their child – demands energy, commitment, courage, a willingness to stick your head above the parapet and risk getting shot at. No one can avoid being marked by that process!

Parents can gain strength in other ways. Many can, and do, group together for mutual support and campaigning. Organisations, such as Mencap, the National Autistic Society, Down's Syndrome Association, Contact a Family, Scope, provide excellent ways in which parents can share experiences, reach common solutions and make connections with one another. Whilst many parents regard such contacts as true lifelines, others (for all kinds of reasons) remain largely detached from mutual support groups. Whether a parent is within or outside such a group, however, he or she largely depends on the attitudes and skills of professionals, together with the policies and resources of the agency they represent, to get the help they need. Some parents are painfully aware of this dependence and its 'cost'. We were discussing vulnerability with a group of parents and the fact that no agency placement can guarantee safety from harm. One mother described her efforts to find an appropriate shared-care placement for her daughter within her local authority. For her, finally, to be able to get short breaks meant the difference between coping and feeling as if she were 'going under.' To question that establishment's ability to protect her child properly seemed to her like 'rocking the boat': she did not want to put the placement at risk. How helpful it would have been, if a worker, or even the agency itself, had sensed this parent's feelings and made it possible for her to be completely open about her hopes and fears.

It is true to say that some parents and professionals can and do work together well and trustingly. As Ruth commented: 'I have been well served by B (a social worker) and the *Barnardos* Team. B was there for me – even at half past seven in the morning. That is often what makes the difference between making it through or not.' Another parent we spoke to felt that 'an outsider' can sometimes see things more clearly and that she is therefore 'open to listening' to other views, including those of professionals.

SEXUALITY: PARENTS AND PROFESSIONALS

We're saying throughout this book that sexuality is a complex, sensitive and usually personal subject. But, because of the reality of the learning disability other people often need to be appropriately involved in the individual's life and decision making. So it is essential that key people, such as parents and professionals, strive to work together and communicate effectively. Because of the power imbalance described above, that we believe the professionals have a responsibility to initiate this process and ensure that it works. We would like to see a move from the scenario on Fig. i (see p. 40) to that of Fig. ii, where parents and professionals are actively trying to establish common ground between themselves. Parents, professionals and the person with learning disabilities her/himself will all have a view on things, and it is only by putting these views together that the picture is likely to be complete (see Fig. iii).

Before seeking to establish all there is in common, parents and professionals each need to ask themselves the following questions:

- First of all, what is my attitude towards people who have a learning disability. Do I really believe they should have a valued presence within my community, with the same human rights that I expect for myself?
- Secondly, what do I think about sexuality, and the right of people who have learning disabilities to a sexual life?

Living and working with people with learning disabilities, parents and professionals will already have a range of deep-seated attitudes and feelings, although not all of these will necessarily be at the front of their consciousness. Clearly, for parents, this sort of

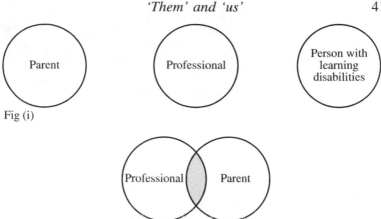

Fig (i)

Fig (ii)

The shaded area represents the degree to which they are working with a common purpose.

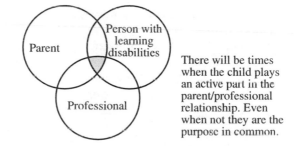

Fig (iii)

There will be times when the child plays an active part in the parent/professional relationship. Even when not they are the purpose in common.

thinking has heavy emotional overtones, in a way that it cannot quite be for professionals, although some professionals are themselves parents of a child with a learning disability. One parent may feel that their main hope is for their child to be cherished within their loving family; another will want as much integration and mixing within ordinary society as possible. Equally, professionals can vary in belief. One will feel that their 'duty of care' is more important than anything else; another will work towards self-determination for their client and certainly view self-advocacy with enthusiasm. We are suggesting that parents and professionals be honest with each other; however, in doing that, each needs to be honest with themselves first.

Many professionals feel strongly about the right of people with learning disabilities to have a sexual life, to be seen as sexual beings. Many parents feel equally strongly that that's wrong. The professional may see unrealised capabilities in the person who has learning disabilities; the parent is more likely to see their vulnerabilities first. What this actually means, however, for each individual person will differ according to their disability and circumstances. It will certainly involve consideration of the following:

- the person's capacity to give meaningful consent
- seeking to establish the person's choices and preferences, whether or not he or she can make the decision for themself
- the degree of support needed to reach appropriate decisions
- who gives that support
- who decides what is 'appropriate'
- in short what is in the 'best interests' of the person, and how that is to be judged and achieved.

These considerations inevitably concern both parents and professionals as well as the person with learning disabilities him or herself, even though each may be setting out from different standpoints.

It is vital that parents and professionals don't see each other as being the 'enemy', but rather acknowledge each other's different contributions to the 'big picture'.

We'll now look at these issues in more detail.

THE RIGHT TO BE SEXUAL AND HAVE A SEXUAL LIFE

There is now a greater understanding and honesty about the previous largely unacceptable conditions in which countless numbers of people with learning disabilities – children and adults alike – once lived. Large-scale hospitals, remote from local communities, were the permanent 'home' of many. It is only within the past 20 years or so that vastly improved policies have brought about closure of these institutions, providing, in their place, care within the community and support for people living within their families. As the changes have progressed and the right to more decent and humane lives has been established, the right to be sexual is gaining attention. Sexual activity most certainly took place in these now redundant hospitals, but on a scale and in a way that was mostly exploitative, non-consenting and abusive. The sexuality of people with learning disabilities wasn't thought of in a positive and affirming way, only as a big problem to be managed and contained. For example, not respecting the need and ability of people even to make and sustain friendships; controlling the fertility of some women with learning disabilities by sterilisation without their understanding or consent to the procedure.

Saying that people with learning disabilities are sexual beings and have a right to a sexual life can be seen as a deeply compassionate response to the injustices of the past. It means moving right away from that place of oppression to one of opportunities and self-determination; it means honouring the right and need of people with learning disabilities to be sexually active, and to participate in sexuality programmes, and to make choices about their bodies and relationships. This view is a practical one, because it responds to the fact that virtually all people grow and develop physically, progress through puberty, and are subject, or potentially subject, to hormones and the feelings they arouse. The time has now come when sex and sexuality matters are rightly out in the open and can no longer be ignored or hidden away. People with learning disabilities have more opportunities for leading fulfilling lives, and sexuality is a natural part of that.

For too long people with learning disabilities have lived without much respect, and that's still partly true. Even if loved and cherished within their families, and receiving a service that really does try to value them, the world 'out there' remains ambivalent about people with learning disabilities. Embarrassment, fear and rejection are still familiar attitudes shown by the general public, and respect cannot feature in those. So the argument for improving the lot of people with learning disabilities is a powerful one. (We shall explore this further in the next chapter).

RIGHTS AND RESPONSIBILITIES OF PARENTS AS PROTECTORS

By 'rights' we mean having power, privileges accorded by law or nature. A number of parental rights are written in law, but most will be accepted as common sense, arising from parents' responsibilities towards the due care and nurture of their child. Parents have rights in regard to their child's education (choice of school), health (giving or withholding permission in relation to a treatment), access to sex education, permission to marry: for such as these there is a legal context. Age is also important here. Sixteen is the age at which someone can legally marry, but parental permission is necessary; at 18 it is not. However, there are many other ordinary rights – for example, the right to choose what TV programmes to watch, bedtime, the amount of pocket money; the right to influence religious and cultural beliefs, and guide moral and ethical development.

In the area of sexuality, most parents will probably feel that they have rights too, but this will also depend upon their child's age. Parents make conscious and subconscious decisions much of the time about how to respond to questions such as, 'How did I get into your tummy?' 'You've got boobies, Mummy. Why hasn't Daddy got any?' As the child gets older, parents are gradually and slowly letting go of some of the control, and beginning to hand it on to their son or daughter – they are beginning to let go of some of their rights. For example: parents may disapprove of their son's choice of friends, but the right to intervene in some way is very different when the child is ten as opposed to 15. A 16-year-old girl has sex for the first time: her parent would have the right to ensure that it is protected sex, but might question whether it is reasonable to do more than check out whether their daughter is freely and knowingly entering into the activity. Much will depend upon the relationship between parent and child and their personal beliefs about sexual activity.

The whole area of sexuality can become a bit of a battleground for parents and their children. Where the child/young person has a learning disability, however, the parent is more than likely to hang on to those rights for much longer, and indeed most parents do so. Some parents will feel that they should never let go. There are very good reasons for this, and they are explored at length in the next two chapters. Basically, it is to do with the fact that people with learning disabilities are vulnerable; there is no way around that fact, and parents are particularly in touch with that reality. On the whole, parents are in a good position to make judgements about their son or daughter's vulnerability and right to a sexual life, because of the special and unique knowledge they have. We say 'on the whole', because some parents, some of the time, will need to be challenged on this subject. This is where the importance of issues such as mutual respect and listening needs to be established by professionals, who are the ones most likely to be the challengers.

One person's rights have to be balanced against another person's, so rights carry responsibilities and have consequences. As Theresa says: 'Max is a unique individual. I feel that I do not have the right to impose my views on him. Yet I am also clear that I need to know that he is safe and not being abused.' In implementing their rights, parents have responsibilities towards their children – ensuring their physical, mental, emotional and spiritual wellbeing, safeguarding them, giving them space to grow and develop, loving them . . . there's no argument here. In the area of sexuality, perhaps, it's clearer to understand what the responsibilities are, as opposed to the rights: responsibilities to ensure they are not harmed, do not harm others, have opportunities to grow, learn to act responsibly themselves.

Parents also have a responsibility to ensure that they exercise their rights in a way which does not harm or diminish their child, and they need to be aware of the consequences of exercising their rights. In saying that she has a right, and a responsibility, to prepare her son Bill for adult life, Jenny also acknowledged that 'He too has rights the same as anyone else but needs some steering because his naivety means he doesn't always understand what the consequences of his actions may be.' So for her, one way of managing the risk that he may have sex, with a resulting pregnancy (which his mother believes he would not have the capacity to manage, not to mention the consequences for the baby), is to teach him that, as a Christian, there is 'no sex until marriage'. She doesn't feel entirely comfortable about this form of control, because it feels, perhaps, to be taking her right to protect too far. She is honest enough to say that it's actually more in response to her fears.

Ruth too has views on this. She says:

> *I think I have the right to be actively involved in decisions about her [Terry's] life. It's debatable as to how much say I or anyone should have. It really depends on the situation. Practically speaking, if the disabled person is still living with you, it affects your life. Your rights are dependent on their disability. We influence them by talking to them the same as we do with our other children.*

And Sandra felt that: 'Parents have no right of veto, but we should have a say in what goes on if it has an effect on the whole family's life.'

Carol, mother of Susannah aged 17, wonders:

> *I should have rights but I don't . . . do I? But if she [Susannah] were to get pregnant, who would bring the baby up? Either I bring up another Down's baby or I have to live with knowing that my granddaughter was being brought up in care where I couldn't give the support I would want to.*

And who really has rights? It may appear to be the parents, but this isn't necessarily how they feel. As Gina, mother of Betty, aged ten, comments: 'What rights do we really have as parents? We feel insecure in this area [of sexuality].'

Many parents are acutely aware of the consequences of their child who has learning disabilities as a sexual person. Much of this is to do with fears that the person will be harmed, will get pregnant or make a girl who also has learning disabilities pregnant, or get involved in sexual activity to which they could not properly consent. It's crucial that professionals are aware that many parents will be fearful about their child's rights with regard to sexuality. The likely consequence will be that they (the parent) may hang on to their own rights (to protect) more firmly than may be really helpful.

PARTNERSHIP: A WAY FORWARD

> *'Agencies have to take the parents on as well as their sons and daughters – not just fob them off. Their concerns are real and often, years later, agencies get in touch with things that have concerned many parents for years.'*
>
> Dino, father of Mark aged 22

During the past two or three decades the importance of participation between people who use services and those who provide them has been seen as increasingly important. The word 'partnership' is heard often, but what does it really mean?

Some ideas put forward by Simon Goldsmith (of Values Incorporated, details at the end of the book) are that partnership is:

- a two-way street, where the partners both give and take
- that each cares what happens to the other
- a working together from the start
- both making an equally valued contribution
- being able to respect different ideas and how each feels
- being able to be open and honest
- understanding each other
- sharing ideas and building together from there.

In other words mutual helping and sharing of the wealth of knowledge, skills and experience each have in common in order to bring about agreed goals.

This requires a move by parents from

- feeling hopeless to hopeful
- self-doubt to self-belief
- thoughts of impossibility to what is possible
- feeling to have little control to feeling in control.

This requires a move by professionals from

- seeing people as obstructive to seeing them as contributors
- expecting little from parents to expecting much,
- a commitment to finding similar aspirations to those of parents.

Recognising that parents' lives are likely to be incredibly busy, he suggests they are given: support, time, and encouragement.

This approach continues by saying that professionals have to learn to share power; to move from traditional approaches to creative ones; to try to move from crisis intervention to preventive work. Importantly, professionals need to admit that they do not necessarily know better; people have different kinds of knowledge, and experts don't necessarily have the answer. Bringing people together in ways that bring about change, through the building of alliances, means that professionals have to continue to develop

- organising skills
- analytical skills
- coalition building,
- and to stay the course alongside parents, to persevere.

This sort of working together depends upon:

- having a shared vision for what can be
- mutual understanding, respect and trust
- those involved seeing that collaboration is in their own interest
- an ability to compromise
- being able to communicate openly, frequently and effectively
- both having a stake in the process and the outcome.

It may be worth professionals and parents considering the idea of a written agreement or contract, which formalises discussions, and makes clear and values the contribution of both parties. Where people with learning disabilities are also part of the discussion, their views should be recorded and taken into account.

Stumbling blocks

There are a number of stumbling blocks to parents and professionals establishing partnership.

Although the separate parties may have similar concerns, they have different questions in mind. Parents say – what about the future? What will happen when we're not there? Is this service safe? Why don't people really understand what it's like for me? Professionals say – what can be done today? Do I have enough resources for this need? What will my manager say if I do this?

Workers move on, so it can be hard for parents to invest in a trusting relationship if they think the person concerned will not be around.

> '*You get fed up with new people. You make strong relationships and when people leave due to whatever – career progression etc. – building new relationships takes energy and you get sick of it. Professionals don't stay around, they move on. Constantly having to build relationships with them is demanding and you lose the energy for it.*'
>
> *Theresa*

Are workers really able to stick with parents when times are tough? Are they able to bear hearing the reality of the pain in the parent's life? 'No.' As Theresa says, 'It's too personal, too enormous. To empathise you have to be on the same level.'

Agency policies and ways of providing services may change, so consistency is lost.

Parents' past experiences of not being accepted as partners and the knowledge that professionals have masters to whom they are accountable don't help either. In practical terms, the stumbling blocks to partnership illustrate gaps between parents and professionals. We now go on to look at some of these.

Gaps between parents and professionals

Many workers see their role as primarily one of enabling; many parents see their role as one of protecting. Therefore workers may view parents as over-protective; parents may view workers as naïve. Equally, many parents look for help and support in responding appropriately to their son or daughter's sexuality but do not know of a worker able to offer it. Just as there are some workers actively promoting the rights of people with learning disabilities to be sexual, other workers feel completely out of their depth. In sensing this, parents may then retreat: it takes effort and determination to get around professional blocks, defences and reluctance.

Some parents can articulate their fears; others are intuitively concerned. Workers must be sensitive especially to the latter and help them to speak out.

Some parents are out of touch with the reality of their daughter/son's life – 'He has no sexual feelings' is often heard. However, many parents are aware of their child as a sexual person, so professionals should take care to distinguish between the two. (There will be some people with learning disabilities who, for whatever reason, do not appear to experience sexual feelings, but they are likely to be a very small minority.)

Parents have unique understanding and insights regarding their child. This knowledge must be sought by professionals and respected.

Professionals are usually very over-stretched and concerned with significant numbers of people; parents are concerned about one.

Parents are more likely to know and/or be in touch with, the consequences of their son/daughter's sexuality should things go wrong and to have to bear those consequences. Are professionals willing to listen?

What is in the best interests of the person with learning disabilities and who is in the best position to determine this? Many if not all decisions made for people with learning disabilities are said to be 'in their best interests', without there being any system for deciding what these best interests actually are. In other words, 'best interests' may be open to differing interpretations and may enable some decision makers to impose their own views of what is right. The Law Society, in a paper called 'Who Decides? (1998), suggests that the phrase should be 'best personal interests' to 'stress that priority should be given to identifying those issues most relevant to the incapacitated individual, rather than to the decision maker or other people'. The challenge for parents and professionals alike is to see if they can agree that making decisions about best interests 'is about encouraging, enabling and supporting the individual learning disabled person to express and make choices, and control what happens in their life'. Difficulty in agreeing this is probably one of the major gaps between parents and professionals. Even if agreement is there in principle, it may be lacking in how the supported decision making is achieved. (See the discussion on Consent, page 61.)

Parents raising the subject of sexuality with professionals

It is a mistake to presume that most parents of children with learning disabilities have their heads in the sand as far as sexuality is concerned. Some mothers think well in advance about how to explain menstruation to their young daughters and help them cope with it on a practical level. Parents who have a young child with autism often understand that what their child learns now has to be appropriate for later adult life. Parents often, too, look for ideas on how to give their child the information she/he needs about keeping safe. We should not presume that such parents are in the minority. Many would welcome help with managing difficult sexual behaviour, such as their son masturbating in the shopping centre, their 13-year-old daughter lifting up her top to show the minibus driver what's underneath, or a nine-year-girl who has always preferred the attention of men and actively seeks them out. Who is there to advise them and offer support?

Professionals raising the subject of sexuality with parents

Those workers who strongly support the right of people with learning disabilities to a sexual life, sexual activity and to information may or may not try to involve parents. Much will depend, for example, on the worker's point of view about the parents' right to be consulted. Age is also relevant, and any debate or query about whether or not parents should be involved can only take place if the person with learning disabilities is an adult. Our view is that parents should be involved, because of the deep knowledge they have of their son or daughter, but we're aware that this is an incredibly sensitive area. Ideally, this should be a three-way process involving the person with learning disabilities, the parent and worker, in order to stand a chance of seeing the bigger picture. If the person is a child, then clearly the parent's view is paramount. However, there is a 'grey area' for young people aged between 16 and 18 where, according to the circumstances of a particular situation, the degree to which parents are involved might be less absolute.

Sometimes it is workers who see the difficulties resulting from an individual's sexuality or sexual behaviour. Workers have approached us with two situations:

- a 16-year-old boy in a school for children with autistic spectrum disorders who was sexually harassing female staff, verbally and by touching
- a 14 year-old boy in a local authority residential establishment for short breaks was masturbating in the lounge while younger children were present.

It is not just the views of the parent, of course, that will affect any sexuality work with a person who has learning disabilities. Both the parent and their daughter or son come from a particular cultural/religious background, and this will inevitably influence their attitudes towards sexuality. Professionals must respect and work with that. Sensitivities arise in being able to talk to parents about such issues as what a sexuality programme consists of, how to respond to a person with learning disabilities who is sexually interested in another (including someone of the same sex), the hygiene routine for menstruation and intimate care where provided, and how to respond to erections and masturbation. Whilst responses to issues such as these may generally be the same across cultures, there will be certain differences which must be understood and respected.

Culture and religion in terms of sexuality and learning disability are very important, complex issues in themselves. We hope that the more general issues raised here will provide a basis on which the more specific issues of culture and religion can be explored and built upon elsewhere.

A WAY FORWARD: THE ASSESSMENT PROCESS

Carrying out an assessment is a structured way of gathering knowledge and information, through which better informed decisions can be reached, and is one way in which parents and professionals can both participate. There already exist structures for certain types of assessment, involving both parents and professionals, although it is the latter who take the lead. Examples are:

- The special educational needs assessment for school placement and identifying accompanying resources
- A social services assessment for a specific service, such as shared care or short breaks
- The '14+ assessment' under the Disabled Persons Act 1986
- The Children Act 1989 recognises the importance of partnership between parents and agencies; therefore the views of parents should always be taken into account during the assessment
- The Carers (Recognition and Services) Act 1995 where a carer (of a disabled child, for example) may request a local authority to carry out an assessment of their needs as carers.

In all these the contribution from parents is actively encouraged because it is recognised that parents have opinions, experience and knowledge of their child that is different from anyone else's. In the social services assessment, the parent's need for support is also recognised as it is within the Carers Act.

Carrying out an assessment could also be a good way for parents and professionals to make progress on matters of sexuality. The assessment would focus on the needs of the person with learning disabilities, which would be identified by pooling the particular knowledge of parents and professionals. Take the example of the 16-year-old boy with autism we described earlier. His teachers might devise a programme of managing his behaviour at school, but that would be incomplete. Does he behave like that at home? If so, how do his parents respond? How much does *he* know or understand about himself as a sexual person and the way his body works? What is his parents' attitude towards him as a sexual person? Without finding the answers to these questions, the picture held by his school is incomplete. A key question to consider is how much is he able to contribute towards the assessment and is he enabled to do so? By consulting his parents, and involving him, other needs may be identified for either of them. If a behaviour management programme is devised it needs to be done in collaboration with parents, as does its implementation, to avoid the young man receiving contradictory messages. If a programme of sexuality work is to be done, that, too, needs to be agreed and delivered in full agreement between home and school.

We have talked about the importance of parents and professionals working more closely together, without, as yet, saying much about the person with learning disabilities as a part of this partnership. This may seem reminiscent of a time when people with learning disabilities were simply passive recipients of services, rather than actively participating in making decisions concerning themselves. It is essential that the person with learning disabilities remains at the heart of the matter and is as fully involved in planning and making decisions as much as is possible for them. This doesn't mean that they participate in all the discussions; just as the person with learning disabilities needs to 'speak' freely without their parent present, so the parent needs the same sort of space in order to speak their truth honestly.

6 People with learning disabilities as sexual beings – rights and realities

Earlier, we said that society had a shameful past in the way that people with learning disabilities had had their human rights denied. Now we see that the pendulum is swinging from that extreme towards the other: from a position where society believed people with learning disabilities had no rights, to one where, some, at least, feel people with learning disabilities should have full rights and access to those rights, with immediate effect. In principle, this is only right and proper. But if we are genuinely to make sure that people with learning disabilities are allowed to exercise full rights in their lives, then this matter requires closer attention.

If people with learning disabilities have a right to be sexual and to have a sexual life, what are the consequences of this for both them and their carers? And, first, what do we mean by 'rights'? Is it just a fancy way of saying 'doing what you please and hang the consequences'? And how can this possibly apply to vulnerable individuals, such as people with learning disabilities?

Ann Craft, whose ground-breaking work on sexuality and learning disabilities helped to open up the whole subject, described the following 'Rights' in relation to people with learning disabilities:

The RIGHT to grow up
The RIGHT to know
The RIGHT to be sexual
The RIGHT not to be at the mercy of the individual sexual attitudes of different care givers
The RIGHT not to be abused
The RIGHT to dignified and humane environments.

The right to grow up

Once people are over 18 they have a right to be treated and valued as an adult, even though their understanding and social functioning may be at a different level to that of a non-disabled person of the same age. Too often people with learning disabilities are seen as eternal children, never entering into adulthood, even though they may live well into old age. This reinforces an individual's degree of dependency, adding the belief that he or she can never progress to achieve some level of self-reliance. The concept of 'letting go' which usually accompanies adolescence may seem unnecessary to parents where their adolescent son or daughter is learning disabled. But all people have the potential for growth and development, provided they are given opportunities and supported through the belief of others that they can succeed. Thinking of people who have a severe learning disability, this attitude can make a positive difference. Opportunities to be involved in seemingly ordinary decisions such as which clothes to wear, which people to be with, what activities to take part in, how personal care is provided, can lead that person towards fulfilling their potential and will certainly build self-esteem.

A school for children with severe learning disabilities used to separate pupils according to ability. So children of eight could be in a class alongside children who were five or six years older. A new head changed the approach by constructing classes more on the basis of age. The immediate benefits for those between 16 and 19 was that their curriculum became more appropriate to their age and stage in life. Staff attitudes also changed, in that it was easier for them to see this group as young people rather than as 'children'.

The right to know

People with learning disabilities have a right to know about everything that is appropriate to help them make the best of themselves, and everything that can enhance their capabilities. This may be about everyday tasks, such as hair washing or making a cup of tea. It most definitely means having knowledge and information that help them function better in their life and relationships. It means having access to facts that they need to know and are ready to receive – for example, names of body parts, how those parts work, and/or possibly sexual relationships.

Too often people with learning disabilities have an assorted collection of accurate facts and misinformation, without necessarily knowing (or having developed the skills to know) which is which. It is also important for an individual to learn about what behaviour is and is not OK. Not knowing or understanding this is all too common for many people with learning disabilities, and this causes difficulties for them and their carers. It can also act as a tangible sign of their vulnerability.

The right to be sexual
They have a right for their sexuality to be affirmed and not denied; to be treated with dignity and respect as a male or female; to be able to look attractive and help choose clothes; to be given appropriate information; to be sexually active – alone or with a partner; to have age-appropriate relationships, including sexual ones if that is right for them; in fact, whatever is appropriate for the individual's ability, age and circumstances.

The right not to be at the mercy of the individual sexual attitudes of different care givers
This is a particular problem for people with learning disabilities who too often hear conflicting messages about sexuality from different people. If the individual has low self-esteem and feelings of powerlessness, then this confusion over what behaviour is 'right' or 'wrong' and what is expected of them can leave them feeling very mixed-up and unhappy. For example, a young man coming to understand that he prefers men as potential sexual partners could be diminished and confused on hearing a mixture of comments that are both pro and anti homosexual relationships. This example was expanded at a consultation meeting with parents to introduce a Sexuality and Relationships Policy. One parent said that he and his wife held conservative values. They felt that sex outside marriage and gay relationships were definitely wrong and also believed in the importance of passing these values on to their children. So a policy that accepted sex outside marriage or homosexual relationships would fly in the face of the values he and his wife had consciously passed to their son. In this situation, whose view should prevail? The answer will have to be ground out within the life and circumstances of those involved.

The right not to be abused

Suffice to say here that people with learning disabilities are particularly vulnerable to all sorts of abuse, both deliberate and as a result of ignorance. The right to be safe from any threat or harm needs therefore to be grasped firmly, together with a clear idea of how that can be achieved. (See Chapter 7 for a fuller discussion.)

The right to dignified and humane environments

This is ultimately about attitudes. Wherever people with learning disabilities are viewed negatively, then the place they are in cannot be dignified or humane. Being treated without respect and consideration diminishes all involved. One of us is a trainer within a local authority for workers on sexuality and people with learning disabilities. Those who are accepted on the course must have previously attended a two-day course called Valued Lives. Valued Lives starts from the principle that people with learning disabilities have the same rights as everyone else, and introduces attitudes, values and ideas which, if taken on by workers, can make a significant difference to the lives of the people they work with. This means that workers who then attend the sexuality and learning disability course have already begun the important task of examining their own views and can, hopefully, appreciate that the provision of dignified environments is a matter of justice and a fundamental requirement in the way services are delivered. There are important lessons here for ALL involved in the lives of people with learning disabilities.

Rights are important for all people, including people with learning disabilities, because they seek to say that each person is of equal worth. Of course, there's no guarantee that societies will go on to treat people as if they are each of equal worth, but it is necessary that a benchmark is set. However, the concept of rights is intensely complex. Rights do not exist in a vacuum: they bring with them responsibilities. An individual should not exert her or his rights unless prepared to accept the consequences of so doing. That's the way human and social life is constructed. Carrying responsibilities means being legally or morally obliged to take care of something or carry out a duty and, in so doing be accountable. This applies to everyone, including people with learning disabilities, although it is by no means straightforward for them.

So let us now look at rights and, perhaps more importantly, consequences, in terms of people with learning disabilities.

Take the right to know, for example. What would be the consequences of this for Steve or Tahir, Jane or Sarai? The answer would be different according to the individual concerned, their age, their circumstances and certainly the level and nature of their disability. Let's say that Steve is someone with a mild learning disability. He has recently become involved with a girl at his day centre and they are engaging in 'heavy petting' sessions at home in his bedroom whenever they get the chance. Steve needs to know about sex and particularly the consequences of having unprotected intercourse with his girlfriend.

Tahir has a profound learning disability. Occasionally when he gets an erection, he strips off all his clothes, irrespective of where he may be. Tahir needs to know that he shouldn't undress in public places. Apart from learning the social codes, he needs to know that this behaviour takes away his dignity.

This is also true of the example given by Gina, mother of Betty aged ten:

> *'our toilet is at the top of a straight flight of stairs and therefore can be seen from the front door. Betty invariably sits on the loo with the door open and can be seen from inside and outside the house, if the front door is open.'*

Before any work on sexuality issues can start with a person who has learning disabilities, it's important to understand the impact on them of being helped to exert their rights. Discussions and decisions need to include parents as the key people in their lives. Because of their knowledge of their son or daughter, parents are more likely to see whether or not exercising rights might lead to some adverse consequences, such as personal harm through exploitation, or taking undue risks. However, as we've said before, the degree to which parents should rightfully be involved will vary from person to person. Again issues such as age, level and nature of the learning disability, the person themself and their circumstances will help determine the amount of parental input. For example, there will be many people with a mild learning disability who are able to make fully consenting decisions about matters to do with sexuality, including having sexual relationships. Others will need help and support in this area – it is not easy to judge who needs help and who doesn't, nor to prescribe what specific help each one will need. It's a case of responding thoughtfully and carefully within each situation. This can be a point of extreme frustration for some parents who are advised to 'let go' or 'loosen up', when in fact their awareness of their son or daughter's vulnerability is what causes them to be so vigilant. They would love to let go but feel that the risks are too great!

Michael and Sally

Michael is 20, has hydrocephalus and attends a further education college. Staff at the college see him as someone who is quietly confident and sure of his own opinions, able to articulate these and his feelings. However, there are times when he seems to lack self-esteem. Staff think he is overprotected but realise his parents see him as vulnerable. The view of some of them is that his vulnerability is a result of being kept 'in cotton wool'. Neither of his parents see it that way. They see that Michael has many gaps in his reasoning ability and that these gaps are masked by his seeming ability. In other words, he appears more aware than he actually is, because he seems to understand things even when he doesn't really.

Sally is aged 18, lives in a group home and has a moderate learning disability. She has serious gaps in her ability but manages many of her own affairs with some help. She is in Michael's group at college. They are keen on each other and want to go out as boy/girlfriend.

What are the issues for Michael and Sally and for the staff who are arguing for their rights?
- That they are adult and have a right to adult relationships
- The college is doing a one-year sexuality programme, giving information about sexual activity, and that this is good for all people because sex education is important for everybody
- Michael and Sally seem to understand that they have responsibilities to each other in a relationship, and Sally has said they will not proceed with anything sexual unless properly prepared, especially with contraception

- The staff say that if things go wrong for Michael and Sally, at least they will have had an opportunity to learn from their experience. All people need a chance to take risks and learn from them.

What are the issues for Michael and Sally's parents?

- That although Michael and Sally are adults, they do have a limited level of understanding. They worry that Michael and Sally will become too involved and not be able to cope.
- The college sexuality work will give information about sexuality and empower the students, but may not be sufficiently flexible to accommodate Michael and Sally's learning needs and specific 'gaps'. Out of a mixture of respect for them and a fear of sounding over the top, they find it hard to explain this properly.
- Sally's parents are not confident that she would be able to negotiate with Michael about what she does and doesn't want in terms of sex. They don't know if Michael and Sally would be able to use condoms properly. They also feel that unless they, as parents, were responsible for Sally's contraception, it would break down and pregnancy might result.
- Sally's parents feel she may be crushed by her experiences if things don't go well. They feel she lives in a world where reality and fantasy intertwine and that the reality of a failed relationship may be something she is unable to recover from.

James and Alex

James and Alex are part of a group taking part in a sexuality programme. They begin to pair off during breaktime in each session with Alex telling the workers that James is her boyfriend. He looks a little uncomfortable when she says this but doesn't disagree. They have no contact with each other between each session, so a relationship never really gets established.

In situations such as James and Alex's, Sally and Michael's, we see people who are both trying to model themselves and their behaviour on what they see the non-disabled world doing and also responding to prompts or urges from within. For various reasons they may not succeed and are, therefore, at risk of hurting themselves or someone else.

'EMPOWERMENT' OR 'VULNERABILITY'?

Those keen to pursue the rights issue need to ask themselves whether giving individuals certain rights (that is, empowering them) may run the risk of increasing their vulnerability. This can become more difficult depending on the degree of the person's disability. If someone has a profound or severe learning disability, then it is easy to see that they are vulnerable and so provide protection accordingly. Where someone is much more able, or appears more able, then it's harder to reach a proper balance between rights and protection. Self-esteem is important here because if disabled persons have a good sense of themselves and their value to others, it's probably easier for them to accept the reality of their learning disability, understand the degree of vulnerability and accept the need for whatever support is appropriate. Let's take Sean as an example.

Sean

His learning disabilities have never been explained in any medical sense, the assumption being that brain damage occurred at or around his birth. Having attended both special and mainstream education he is now in a supported work placement. Until adolescence he was not able to understand or put into words his sense of being different from his peers, nor have his family been able fully to explore this with him because it is so painful. Sean joined a group doing sexuality and self-esteem work. In the sessions, the workers acknowledged with Sean that he had a learning disability and did so in a positive way, not labelling or stigmatising him. Doing this helped Sean come to terms with the reality of his situation. And gaining that understanding helped his self-confidence by taking away any sense of blame or personal responsibility. In conversation with the workers, Sean's mother pointed out that empowerment must be based on a realistic awareness of each person's potential, and to acknowledge, not deny their limitations and need for support.

CONSENT

This is a particularly complex issue for people with learning disabilities and no more so than in relation to sexuality. Consent is about having choices, making decisions, understanding what's involved, and having an awareness of the consequences. No wonder it is fraught with difficulties. However, the presence of a learning disability doesn't mean a person should be prevented from making decisions. The questions worth considering are:

- First, does the person have knowledge/understanding of the issue or situation, plus the confidence and ability to make clear what their wishes really are?
- Secondly, how is the person to be enabled to have their say, and what support is required to enable that decision to be truly self-determined?

If any of the elements in the first are absent, then the carer/s may need to consider suspending the person's right to consent, at least for the interim. This, however, presents a dilemma because, doing so may be unjust, inappropriate and a misuse of power. Fundamentally, there is for parents and carers a tension between their duty of care and wish to respect an individual's right and desire to choose. It all depends on the individual concerned and the situation in question.

Where there is uncertainty for a parent or workers, there are two things that could be considered:

- Assessing the risk. This assessment can be formal, rather like the process commonly used where there are health and safety issues. It can also be approached informally, where the pros and cons of the activity are weighed up and a judgement made about whether one is more significant than the other.
- Looking at comparable areas of the person's life in which making decisions, consenting and self-protection occur. This will help towards making the judgement regarding risks, because there is a guide already as to how the person usually responds.

Parents and carers may need to consider whether they discourage the disabled person from making decisions, because they fear the consequences of what they think could be a wrong decision. Also, there will be times when they, the parent, make a decision on behalf of their child without involving them in that decision. Of course, there will be times when that is right; but equally times when it isn't. For example, Kim says: 'for a while Tina was on the pill but not now. I did it for my peace of mind then came to see that that was not a good enough reason'.

The following extract is taken from the guideline on consent in sexual relationships which is part of the Sex, Sexuality and People with Learning Disabilities Policy of Bradford:

> Consent is crucial in deciding whether a particular sexual relationship or act is abusive. What needs to be decided is,
> * whether consent was *able* to be given and,
> * whether it *was* given by the individual.

But of course even that isn't straightforward. Let's take the situation of Vicky.

Vicky

She is 19 years old. Like many people with learning disabilities, Vicky is quite able to comprehend some issues which seem complex whilst finding it hard to understand other simpler things. Vicky has recently started going into a shared care establishment for occasional weekends. Last weekend, a worker found her in bed with Raj, another service user.

What might some of the issues be for Vicky in terms of consent?
* Is she wishing to be with Raj or acquiescing with his wishes?
* If she makes it clear she wants to have sex, why should anyone disagree, and who has the right to make that judgement?
* Do her parents have any rights in this situation?
* If her parents do not have rights, does anybody else?
* Does Vicky understand the risks and the consequences of a sexual relationship?
* Does anybody have the right to discuss the morality of the situation with her, such as casual sexual encounters versus a faithful and stable relationship?
* If it's felt that Vicky can consent to this relationship, does this mean she can consent to all potential sexual encounters? If she is ever approached by someone who appears to have 'bad intentions', how might she respond?

In Vicky's case there may be clear answers to one or two of the above questions. But the very fact that so many queries are possible shows that this is by no means a straightforward situation.

Guidelines produced in 1995 by the Law Society and British Medical Association argue that, in order to consent to sex, a woman must understand what is involved and be able to exercise choice. If we're saying that understanding is needed before consent is given, not just to sex but to other activities or actions, the following questions arise:

- Is partial understanding good enough, or is full understanding required?

  The answer probably depends on the activity proposed, with whom, and especially any risk associated with it. The greater the risk or possibility of adverse consequences, the more important it is that there is a good level of understanding within the person.

- Who assesses whether the individual does have sufficient understanding? Should it be one person with a particular angle on that individual's life, such as a parent, or perhaps two or three each with their own perspectives who, together, will provide a fuller picture than each would on their own? And what if there is disagreement between them; how is that to be managed?

- How is the person with learning disabilities to be involved in this process?

  One way forward is by an approach called 'supported decision making' which is referred to on page 50. There we refer to a Law Society paper, quoted in a publication called *Choice and Control* (1998). For a fuller discussion of this approach and the complexities of consent, this is well worth reading.

RIGHTS AND RESPONSIBILITIES

We have said that rights do not exist in isolation, they carry responsibilities, but if a person with learning disabilities does not have the cognitive ability to make responsible decisions about his or her sexuality, then such a person may be placed in extremely vulnerable, unsafe and dangerous situations. This is particularly so if he or she is then expected to act responsibly without being prepared.

By 'responsible' we mean that people are able to understand the nature of the task or role they are carrying out, appreciate the consequences or outcomes and be able to account for their actions.

TAKING RISKS

How do we know if a person with learning disabilities is able to act responsibly in a given situation, unless we give them opportunities to do so? This is a perfectly good question. Taking risks is one way people learn. Without taking risks that are up to, and occasionally beyond, our level of competence, there would be no human or individual progress. Most people learn to accept responsibility by gradually taking on increasingly difficult tasks and challenges, and by reflecting on how well, or not well, they were done in order to do them better next time. It could be said that most real learning is done outside the 'comfort zone'.

This is one approach to risk taking, that if there's no pain, there's no gain. In terms of adults with learning disabilities, there is a belief that unless such people are able to take some risks in their life, they cannot move forward and take their rightful place in the adult world.

The second approach is that risks need managing, possibly reducing rather than expanding. In a way risk taking is something that parents are calculating all the time with their children as they grow up, starting with very small risks and then increasing them as seems appropriate. In reality, the risks that non-disabled children take in later adolescence and early adulthood are often far bigger than parents might wish them to take, but there is probably little they can do in the matter. The growing/grown up 'child' has decided to take the law into his or her own hands! With people with learning disabilities this often isn't the case. They often live within protected environments and do not hold the power; they cannot challenge the *status quo* in the way non-disabled teenagers do. What makes many if not most people with learning disabilities particularly vulnerable is that they do not possess a sufficient degree of insight. Most people generally learn from taking risks because they are able to reflect on the experience, evaluate the outcome and make a decision about how to deal with the same or a similar situation should it arise again. Those with profound learning disabilities are not likely to possess the ability or skill to reflect or evaluate. Those who have a mild learning disability may possess a degree of insight which aids their learning from taking risks and having new experiences as long as these are carefully weighted. However, this same insight may enable them to see or sense that they are not accepted as being equal with their non-disabled peers. A subsequent desire to 'do anything to be liked' leaves them more vulnerable to abusive relationships. Even for those who have good self-esteem; it may be found that it's not enough to protect them in vulnerable situations if it's not accompanied by an adequate degree of insight and ability to judge wisely. Because many parents and workers are well aware of these difficulties, the reality of risk taking for many people with learning disabilities is that it is something decided upon by others, who perhaps veer more towards control than support, safety rather than trying out.

Parents and risk taking

Parents will often be fearful that gradual risk taking cannot be the same with their daughter or son who has learning disabilities, as it is with their non-disabled children. They need to be sure that professionals fully appreciate this, especially where sexuality is concerned. And, if sexuality work is proposed, workers should know the importance of breaking the information down into small manageable parts, if unacceptable risks are to be avoided when the learning is applied in real life. Responding to and managing risk within the area of sexuality is a difficult thing to achieve, because so much of it is a personal part of life and, if we truly respect the rights of people with learning disabilities, is it really appropriate, for example, to watch over someone if a relationship is developing? It would seem to go against all natural dignity and respect. This is the case even if the couple are only making small talk and chatting each other up. Even to be party to that would seem voyeuristic. To be around, or watching, if the couple were doing anything overtly sexual, would seem quite wrong. So there is a real difficulty over how responsibly and respectfully workers and parents can help or enable their sons or daughters to achieve greater independence, including sexual independence. Yet if we do not protect appropriately, there are real risks that the person's behaviour may have consequences from which they, and their parents, may not recover. The situations that spring to mind are always the worst examples, the 'nightmare scenarios' such as the sexual exploitation of a person with learning disabilities by someone without learning disabilities, or the relationship that leads to an unwanted pregnancy or a sexually transmitted infection. It's important not to under-estimate the potential for harm and sadness.

However, there may be other less complex consequences: for example, a relationship which comes to an end. Those involved may feel the hurt of rejection or loss more severely than a person without learning disabilities, and may have great difficulty in recovering from it. This is not to say that relationships should not be entered into; after all, most of us have 'loved and lost', that's part of what makes us individual and shapes our personality. But it is necessary to acknowledge that people with learning disabilities may already have experienced a variety of rejections in their life, so the ending of a relationship can be even more traumatic.

BECOMING SEXUAL

> *'Bill always wanted to have a girlfriend. At [mainstream] school he had girls as friends only; attempts to go beyond that were rebuffed. Occasionally Bill says, "I wish I didn't have Down's Syndrome".'*
>
> *Jenny*

Should an experience such as Bill's mean that people with learning disabilities should not be seen as sexual beings with potential, because of the sometimes unhappy consequences that arise? And at what point does anyone become a sexual person anyway? Some would say that puberty is the defining point, when the body changes and there is no denying the emergence of adulthood. Others might argue that it's a mental process: there is a moment when both body and mind grow, mature and develop understanding and awareness of being sexual. And yet, even when we are talking about children, we see that their behaviour can show evidence of sexuality long before they start playing at 'doctors and nurses'. Baby boys have erections, even male babies in the womb have erections. This is not to say that they are having sexual feelings in the way that an adult would experience sexual arousal, but in a way this shows the complexity of what we are talking about: the physical mechanics of the human body. It's as though nature is determined to put the physical ability to procreate as a top priority.

Some parents will say that their son or daughter who has a learning disability does not have sexual feelings. There will be the occasional individual to whom this appears to be true, but in general there will be few people who do not have some notion of at least being attracted to another individual, even if it is only a matter of saying 'He/she's nice'.

Even in people with profound learning disabilities, the biological evidence of sexuality is there, in the simple and undeniable presence of erections and semen in men, and menstruation in women.

The more that people with learning disabilities are empowered, the more likely it is that at least some will want to find meaningful ways of expressing their sexuality. People with learning disabilities are often very quick to pick up covert messages given by their parents or carers, and because they are often conditioned to be compliant they are more likely to do what is asked of them. So, if the message says, 'You will not have sexual feelings', or 'You will not display sexual behaviour', or 'You will not enter into a sexual relationship', then people with learning disabilities may well try to adhere to this, or at least try to conceal what they really feel and/or do.

When the message given by parents or other people is repressive, this may have profound implications for the person with learning disabilities. When sexuality is denied or the right to be sexual repressed, then the individuals concerned may feel that their whole humanity is being squashed. This will certainly have negative impacts for the people concerned, and could lead to mental ill health, or even the forming of 'unhealthy' sexual behaviour.

Michael

Michael is a 44-year-old man who has learning disabilities living in a hostel. Michael has never received any teaching on sex or sexuality. When he began collecting pictures of people in underwear from clothing catalogues, staff weren't particularly concerned about this and let him get on with it. Michael is a friendly person but rather reserved and finds it difficult to make friends or acquaintances. He is very good at getting on with children. He regularly visits his local park and takes sweets to share with the children. He has become quite a feature in the park, trusted by all the children and their parents, who see him as 'the kindly disabled man from next door'. One Saturday he is arrested by the police for taking three children (all under ten) into the park toilets to 'look at their bits'. (They ran away before he could get them to undress). Michael is later released without charge. Back at home the staff look into his collection of pictures and find that Michael also has several scrapbooks in which he has pasted pictures of young children. They are modelling nightwear, underwear and sports clothes, such as shorts and swimming costumes.

Is Michael's sexual activity unhealthy? Is it the confused actions of a person with learning disabilities who doesn't know enough about behaving properly? Or is there a serious crime waiting to happen?

Professionals in health and social services departments work with many adults with learning disabilities whose behaviour verges on the unsafe and illegal. There are many reasons why each person is in that situation, and a key one is likely to be that their need and right to be acknowledged as sexual beings has not been afforded them.

Finally, in terms of sexuality, it is essential that people with learning disabilities are given the opportunity to make their own decisions. This does not mean they will always be able to make decisions without support, but it does mean that any decisions made about their lives, which do not include their opinions, will be unjust and will ultimately fail. Giving people with learning disabilities the opportunity to express preference and exercise as much autonomy as possible in making decisions, will help develop their self-esteem, and so give them a healthier, more positive view about themselves, and hopefully reduce the risks associated with making relationships.

7 Learning disability and vulnerability

When we use the term 'learning disability', we tend to think of a particular group of people. However, in reality, learning disability is a continuum or spectrum of people ranging from those with mild disabilities who live significantly in the mainstream of life without receiving formal support from service agencies, through to those with profound disabilities who are very dependent and need total care. Therefore, the amount of support that people with learning disabilities will need, for example, to make decisions regarding their personal life will vary according to who they are and what their individual needs are. It's important that we don't generalise about people's abilities in terms of mental capacity. There will be, for example, some people who do not know how to use money, but this doesn't mean that they don't understand what staff members they can trust. Ability to judge or not judge, or ability to judge in one area doesn't prove ability to judge in another: 'There is no single definition of mental capacity; there is no one right method of assessing mental capacity; each case has to be dealt with on its own circumstances' (Cheeseman, D., in Walsh, B., 1994, page 67).

We all arrive in this world vulnerable and dependent on others for our very life and safekeeping. In that sense all people are equal in their dependency. For parents of newborn babies, the desire to protect and nurture is normally very strong, almost overwhelming. As the child grows, however, the parent learns to lighten up, although never quite losing the sense of keeping a watchful eye open, even when the 'child' has children of their own. Where the child has a learning disability, the desire to protect runs very deep indeed. It is an intuitive recognition as well as an intellectual understanding of the reality of the learning disability. And there is a gut feeling that the vulnerability is there for good. How common it is to hear many parents say, 'What will happen to my child when I am gone?'

It might help to start by defining vulnerability. Dictionary definitions say 'vulnerable' means being open to harm or attack; susceptible to being wounded. Harm, attack, wounded – these are hard words to contemplate, because of the fearful images they conjure up in our minds, as parents. But if we are to do anything about reducing their effects and managing their realities we have to face them.

> *'They would probably go with anyone. If asked to take their clothes off they would probably do it and of course it worries me when you hear of people targetting people with learning disabilities in residential homes. The boys wouldn't know they were being abused'.*
>
> *Sandra, mother of Jack 33 and Tim aged 24*

In all discussions about sexuality and people with learning disabilities, vulnerability cannot be ignored, and our argument is that professionals and workers must own up to it in the way that parents do every second of every day. Doing so will allow all of us to move forward in creating lifestyles that offer maximum opportunity for personal growth, development and enjoyment, whilst at the same time minimising the risk of harm.

VULNERABILITY VARIES

In addition to external factors, the degree to which an individual person with learning disabilities is vulnerable depends on a number of elements – the nature and extent of the learning disability itself, age, temperamental makeup, how he or she has been or is being brought up, level of confidence and self-esteem. Labels are, at best, clumsy, particularly when grouping people with a wide range of life experiences together as a 'type'. It may seem simplistic and demeaning to do so and not reflect the intricacies and individuality of the person. However, we have used the following groupings as a way of conveying what we need to say in order to try to define disability in respect of vulnerability.

Mild-moderate learning disability

Here the person is living almost or fully independently, and making or sharing in decisions about such matters as clothing, money, social events, friendships and relationships. Many adults with very moderate learning disabilities live with minimal support and in many ways cope well. However, the vulnerability that is part of their learning disability is often only too visible to other people, who may set out to take advantage of them in some way.

Examples of this could be: a person with learning disabilities living alone who was being persuaded or harassed into handing over money; a man with learning disabilities 'agreeing' to sex in a public toilet; a woman with learning disabilities being drawn into an abusive sexual relationship. Once again self-esteem is absolutely crucial. The person who looks unkempt, moves and walks hesitatingly, or finds it hard to maintain eye contact wears vulnerability on his or her sleeve. Conversely, the self-confident person is likely to move about purposefully, look relaxed and easy and be personally presentable. They are less vulnerable anyway and the vulnerability that is there is far less obvious. The Suzy Lamplugh Trust, which gives guidance on personal safety for anyone, describes how this can be enhanced by being alert – walking tall, keeping your head up and looking confident. So there is a message here for all people.

Severe disability

Between the mild-moderate and profoundly learning disabled ends of the spectrum, this is probably where the majority of people whom society sees as having learning disabilities fit. The degree to which each person is vulnerable depends on some of the factors we mentioned earlier – cognitive impairment, life history and experience, the level of self-esteem and assertiveness, the ability to relate to others, personal presentation, flexibility in responding to the unexpected and, importantly, the support network.

Feeling good about oneself is a crucial ingredient in self-protection. For example, Kim's daughter Tina is a sports champion within her own field. She knows herself to be skilled and able. Winning gives her a great boost. Having a learning disability still means she is vulnerable, but her talents in one particular area increase self-confidence and also her social status because of her personal achievements. We're not saying that high self-esteem in one area of the life of a person with learning disabilities always means they are less vulnerable. The opposite is possible in that high self-esteem may mean a person thinks of himself as being less vulnerable than he really is, which is just another example of how complex this whole subject is.

Profound and multiple learning disability
The vulnerability is only too easily evident. The person clearly has a high degree of physical dependence and need for constant watchfulness. Such severe disabilities are often accompanied by additional impairments of hearing and sight. In these circumstances, such people will not be able to protect themselves effectively, but that doesn't mean that nothing can be done to make the most of what is possible with them. It can. A consistent and continuing programme could look at areas such as: carers consciously giving them everyday choices, encouraging them to indicate clearly what they like and dislike; their personal presentation and self-awareness, their being aware of what touch feels safe and what unsafe; their working on ways of indicating 'yes' and 'no'; their having a consistent routine to help them be able to anticipate events, and therefore any changes that may occur. We say more about this in Chapter 8. However, the key responsibility for protecting has to lie with other people – parents, carers and organisations.

'ABUSE' AND 'aBUSE'

In our work with parents, we have seen that knowledge of their child's vulnerability is uppermost in their minds – see Chapter 5. And most parents when encouraged to say what that means, will qualify it as vulnerability to sexual abuse. While many 'out there' still deny, or hesitate to accept, that people with learning disabilities can be and are sexually abused, most parents are only too aware of the possibility, if not the reality. It is an ingrained fear that contributes to a way of life, that many professionals all too readily label 'over-protection'. Hard as it is, it has to be acknowledged that there are many ways in which people with learning disabilities are vulnerable, and sexual abuse is only a part of this wider vulnerability. Abuse can be defined in two distinct ways: abuse (with a small 'a') and Abuse (with a capital

A). Both involve the misuse of power. Children with learning disabilities are particularly prone because there are a significant number of power imbalances in their lives, in the same way that there are for women with learning disabilities.

'abuse'

Is it any wonder?
If you leave the door open when you're changing me
or bring Sonia in and 'do her at the same time' . . .

If you talk to your friend Hilary
And 'do' me at the same time . . .

If you look through me like I'm not there
And chat to your mate about last evening's telly
And you expose my private hair
And leave me uncovered from me toes to me belly
And you cough and splutter and say 'phwor, this one's
*   smelly' . . .*

Is it any wonder . . .
*   That I believe myself to have no worth? . . .*
*   That is what you believe*
*   And grown ups are right and can be trusted.*

Is it any wonder . . .
*   That I don't understand words like 'dignity' and*
*   'privacy'*
*   When I've not been shown or given any?*

Is it any wonder . . .
*   That I don't scream or cry, moan or complain*
*   When the new worker does things to me for which I*
*   know no name*
*   And when he says 'It will be OK – and if it's not then*
*   you'll be blamed'*
*   – You know he's right, cos grown ups are always right,*
*   and can be trusted.*

Is it any wonder I won't eat my food
'She won't even touch her apple crumble' . . .
And I bang my head against the wall instead
– so hard, the plaster crumbles.

John Drury

So, 'abuse' may be subtle and goes on much of the time. It could be called simply poor practice although may be worse than that. It may not be easily recognised as 'abusive', although anyone observing it may experience a bit of discomfort. In her book, *Proud Child, Safer Child*, Merry Cross defines abusive practice as: 'any practice which is profoundly disrespectful of a person as a human being . . . it is practice based on assumptions that are false and contemptuous'. The assumptions are 'that what happens to disabled children is less important than what happens to non-disabled children'. Good-quality organisations are constantly looking at how they can do better in the way they provide their service; seeking to improve standards and clarifying what they mean by 'good practice'. However, there are still too many examples of poor practice in our day services and residential establishments, and much of this could be called 'abusive'. For example, it is all too easy for workers feeding children to talk to one another rather than giving that child their full attention. The workers may even talk about the child as if she or he were simply an object and not a flesh-and-blood creature with feelings. As the poem above shows, joky banter, even if arising from staff embarrassment, is not good practice. Organisations have a responsibility to ensure that all their staff are practising to the highest possible standards. We talk further about this in Chapter 9.

Another example is of the child who has problems with his or her behaviour being viewed as 'a problem' rather than the behaviour itself receiving the attention. It's worth workers and parents looking at the possibility that problem behaviour may be the only way that the child can communicate that something that is wrong or making them confused or unhappy.

Poor practice can occur in intimate care by the way a person with learning disabilities is handled. Haste, a lack of gentleness and certainly inattention to something as basic as privacy all run the risk of being harmful, if not physically then certainly psychologically. It's worth thinking about how we would like personal care to be given, and, in fact, some of us may have experienced that whilst in hospital. How much better it is when a professional is respectful, takes the time to explain what is going to happen and listens to our questions and anxieties, where a procedure is done as carefully as possible and when our dignity is preserved. This should be the experience of all people and especially so if dependence on others is permanent.

There may be times when a particular practice is done with the intention of punishing a child or adult, or is allowed to be an expression of a worker's feelings. So someone using a communication board has it removed for a time; there is delay in taking them to the toilet, or having their pad changed; someone is deliberately left to cry or rock or bang their head; a person is verbally harassed or demeaned, and even if the words don't carry a meaning, the tone of voice certainly will. As parents and workers, we all get tired and short-tempered at times. It's important to admit that so that we can anticipate 'bad practice' and do all we can to avoid it. And if anyone finds him or herself having done it, it's important to admit one is out of order and to apologise. That way you restore the person's self-esteem and certainly learn a vital lesson for yourself. Agencies have a key role here in making clear to staff what is good practice and what is abusive practice. There is much they can do through policies, guidelines, staff training and support/supervision to encourage all to work towards the best standards of service delivery possible. This issue must be recognised and taken seriously.

Parents, too, can find themselves in danger of being abusive, although that may be the last thing on their minds. This can happen if a parent has low expectations of their child, so keeping him or her cocooned from risks and stifling their growth. Children who learn at school to communicate via Makaton or BSL (British Sign Language) signs depend on their parents to become familiar with the method also; some parents cannot or will not do so, and thereby risk losing the chance of developing meaningful communication with their son or daughter, who certainly loses out on an opportunity to reinforce what is being learned. Parents may remove their child's hearing aid the minute they come home from school. Disability benefits can be used for purposes other than the child's well-being. Being a parent of a child with learning disabilities is enormously demanding and generates all sorts of stress. Other factors may also put on the pressure – such as relationship problems within the family, the main earner's loss of employment, other money worries, lack of support – these and more can affect parents' ability to cope and manage their child's needs as well as they would wish. Very few parents set out to harm or diminish their child in any way, but circumstances sometimes make it really hard for them to do as well as they would like. Hard as this is for those parents to face, it is very important that they do so.

All parents and workers need to see that, apart from the harm abuse does to the person with learning disabilities, it can, very dangerously soften up the person to really nasty 'Abuse'. It may also soften up worker/carers, by blunting their sensitivities, so that they see the person with learning disabilities as more of an object and less of a person. This type of practice is the ideal environment for serious Abuse to take hold.

'Abuse'

It is increasingly accepted that people with learning disabilities are vulnerable to physical, mental, emotional and sexual abuse. Books, current research, media reports of abuse in this or that establishment, anecdotal evidence: all clearly dismiss the notion that being disabled is a protection, because, surely, no one would want to harm or target a person with learning disabilities. The opposite is now known to be true. Disability actually provides unique opportunities for potential abusers, particularly those who abuse sexually. Why is this so?

These are some of the reasons:

- the general impression still given by society that disabled people are worth less than non-disabled people
- as a consequence, a person with learning disabilities is likely to have a low sense of self-esteem, and therefore feel deep within him or herself a sense of being less important than others, that he or she matters less
- personal and intimate care is usually provided by a number of different people
- many people from different agencies are usually involved in the child or adult's life
- most children and adults with learning disabilities have no, or only limited, control over their life, so lack experience in building up self-reliance and handling calculated risks

- compliance and obedience tend to be seen by carers as good, so the person with learning disabilities picks up the message that resistance is not encouraged
- the majority of children and adults with learning disabilities receive little or no input on sexuality or keeping safe
- a belief still remains that people with learning disabilities are not targeted for abuse. One consequence of this is that a sign, such as changed behaviour or sexualised behaviour, in a child or adult may be put down to their disability rather than the possibility of abuse
- where a child or adult has a very limited 'vocabulary', whether verbal, signed or a particular communication system, he or she may not be able to indicate or describe what is happening. He or she may not, for example, have been given the right 'words' to enable him or her to do so
- where the child may have limited understanding about his or her own body, (s)he will be less likely to interpret correctly the inappropriateness of sexual acts towards them.

Just as parents can be caught up in 'abuse', so too are a small minority of parents 'Abusers' of their child who has a learning disability. Unpalatable though it is, not all parents, whether deliberately or due to some other factor, seek to protect their disabled child.

What do we know about the sexual Abuse of people with learning disabilities and those who perpetrate it?
It's important to say what is meant by the term 'sexual Abuse'. In her book *Proud Child, Safer Child*, Merry Cross uses a definition taken from *Working Together under the Children Act 1989*:

> SEXUAL ABUSE   Actual or likely sexual exploitation of a child or adolescent. The child may be dependent and/or developmentally immature.

A second definition was drawn up by two researchers, Hilary Brown and Vicky Turk, who undertook the largest UK incidence survey, at that time, of the sexual abuse of adults with learning disabilities. The first part of the research was a retrospective survey of all new cases of sexual abuse reported in 1989 and 1990 in one particular Regional Health Authority. The survey was repeated for the years 1991 and 1992. Brown and Turk (1994) defined the acts involved in sexual abuse as follows:

NON-CONTACT ABUSE

Looking, photography, indecent exposure, harassment, serious teasing or innuendo

CONTACT ABUSE

Touch, e.g. of breast, genitals, anus, mouth; masturbation of either or both persons; penetration or attempted penetration of vagina, anus, mouth with or by penis, fingers, other objects

This may be hard for you to read. We have made a finely balanced judgement about whether to include it. Sexual abuse is one of those terms that signifies something horrible, but we don't necessarily like to dwell on what it means. By being so specific and defining it, our logic is that it will move the subject from a dark hidden place out into the light. To do so is often a very empowering process.

It is not necessarily straightforward to decide whether a particular sexual act between two adults is actually abusive. Judgements are influenced by factors such as how the victim experienced the encounter, the perceived intentions of the perpetrator – his understanding of the situation and whether the victim appeared to him to give consent. Other considerations are the social codes of behaviour that they are accustomed to live by, the nature of the relationship within which it has occurred, and the status of the perpetrator in relation to the victim.

From Brown and Turk's research (1995) it was concluded that:

• Most abusers are male (but evidence shows there are some female abusers).

• Some abusers are people with learning disabilities.

This last point is perhaps hard for you to contemplate, because we are accustomed to seeing people with learning disabilities as invariably victims. But if we think of much sexual abuse as being related to power differences, then we can see that many people with learning disabilities (an able man for example), may have more power than some others, such as a young child or a less able woman or man with learning disabilities. There is yet more to be understood about sexual abuse and those who commit it, including people with learning disabilities. However, there are certain elements in the lives of people with learning disabilities that may mean abuse is the outcome, even if it were not intended. Many adults with learning disabilities who grew up in institutions experienced abuse from both staff and other people also with learning disabilities. Without opportunities (and for some, the ability) to reflect on whether this was right or wrong, the abuse may have remained unrecognised for what it was by both perpetrator and victim. Other people with learning disabilities who abuse may never have received clear messages and information about sex, sexuality and sexual behaviours. Without this framework, it is very difficult for a person to know how to manage their sexual drive in a responsible fashion. Even today most people with learning disabilities do not receive good, clear and consistent messages about sex and sexuality. So is it any wonder that some find themselves in situations where their behaviour is questionable, inappropriate or even actually abusive? (This is not to excuse individuals who are abusing others, but an attempt to try to explain why it is the case.) It is important that parents, carers and workers bear in mind that where sexuality is repressed or denied, it is likely that the individual concerned will face unhappiness and confusion which, for some, may express itself in various ways such as sexual offending. It's also worth mentioning the sort of sexual behaviour that may initially be at the thin end of the wedge.

Jon and Marie

Jon is 28, has a moderate to severe learning disability; Marie is a little younger. She has Down's Syndrome and is less able. Both attend the same day centre. Jon has a reputation for 'liking the girls'. Marie is genuinely affectionate and is attracted to Jon. She enjoys holding hands with him and being kissed. As the weeks pass, her parents notice a change in her behaviour; she also starts wetting the bed. It turns out that Jon had had sex with Marie on several occasions. Her behaviour suggests that she doesn't have a proper understanding of what was happening.

Did Marie give meaningful consent to what was happening? Did Jon think she was giving consent and, if not, was he abusing her?

- Most abusers are already known to their victims. They come from four main groups – staff/volunteers, family members (including parents), other trusted adults from within the community such as neighbours, and other people with learning disabilities. But there are still situations where some people with learning disabilities are targeted by people unknown to them.
- Males as well as females are sexually abused.
- Sexual abuse is likely to be systematic rather than a single event – so an individual may be sexually abused many times over a long period and possibly by more than one person.
- Abuse takes place in services such as residential establishments and shared living environments, just as it does within family settings.

From their findings Brown and Turk suggest an incidence figure of over 800 new reported cases of sexual abuse of adults with learning disabilities per annum in England and Wales. In reality, there will be a higher incidence than that, because of a failure to see that it is happening, of it being seen but not reported, or if reported not acted upon and therefore not recorded.

These harsh realities are profoundly depressing and for those individuals who are abused in any way it must be deeply painful. Such realities can and do shock us so much it may be easier to try to ignore them, to freeze them out of our consciousness. However, it is important to remember that there are many people who have not been sexually abused, are not being sexually abused, and never will be. Within that, the key question for every parent is: 'What is the chance of MY child being harmed in any way, and what can I do to keep the odds on it happening as low as possible?'

There are a number of things that individual parents and agencies can and are doing. The following are constructive suggestions for all concerned.

PROTECTING DISABLED CHILDREN AND ADULTS FROM ABUSE

Agencies
Many agencies still need to increase their understanding and awareness of the abuse of disabled children and adults, and the

factors that augment their vulnerability. In a number of books, articles and reports in recent years, social services departments have been criticised for not bringing together child protection workers and workers who specialise in disability in more effective ways. If the two remain separate, who has the expertise to respond appropriately to a disabled child who is being abused? It is not helped by the fact that acquiring reliable statistics on abuse is made harder because the Department of Health does not require social services departments to record disability in their child protection figures. It is therefore difficult to be sure about the extent of sexual abuse of children and young people with learning disabilities. There is a further area in which much needs to be done: agencies should draw up and implement key policies, such as those on sexuality and personal relationships, consent, risk taking, intimate care, sexuality work and the protection of vulnerable adults, together with guidelines. Child care agencies must have a protection policy and guidelines, but the same provision for adults with a learning disability has up until now only been advisory. However, in March 2000, the Department of Health issued a document called *No Secrets – Guidance on Developing and Implementing Multi-agency Policies and Procedures to Protect Vulnerable Adults from Abuse.* Social services departments are required to co-ordinate this new strategy, drawing on all relevant agencies from the statutory, voluntary and private sectors. The document says that the agencies' primary aim should be to prevent abuse where possible but, if the preventive strategy fails, agencies should ensure that robust procedures are in place for dealing with incidents of abuse.

All policies and guidelines should be written in a style that is clear, practical and rooted in the way the service is provided to people with learning disabilities. In other words, the drawing up of policies and guidelines should not be an academic exercise, nor should documents languish on a high shelf out of reach. They have to be workable and grounded in a simple and clearly worded belief in the value of people with learning disabilities as unique individuals who deserve to be viewed with respect, and receive the very best possible service.

There are two main reasons for having policies in place.

First, those receiving services will benefit from making the nature of good practice and how it is to be upheld explicit. There should be no place for sloppiness or ambiguity. For instance, a protection policy will set out the principles that guide its formation and implementation, make clear what constitutes abuse, list the likely signs and signals of abuse and explain clearly the procedures staff must adopt, should they suspect or discover abuse, or have it disclosed to them. In addition, policies need to be placed within the appropriate legal framework and be subject to regular review. Policies, of course, are more likely to be effective and acceptable, if those most likely to be affected – staff, parents/carers and people with learning disabilities – have been widely consulted themselves.

Secondly, if effective policies and guidelines exist, staff will benefit. If good practice is made clear to them and guidance given for tricky situations, individual workers should feel more secure, better valued and consequently do a better job. Also, abusive and potentially abusive staff will be given a clear message that 'We're on the lookout for you', which should be a substantial deterrent.

We now live in a time of service commissioning and purchasing, of care plans and case management. Many parents have already experienced this, as have their sons and daughters. It means that social services departments and health trusts are no longer the sole provider of services such as day activities, residential care and the like. A person with learning disabilities may experience a package of care that involves two or possibly three different agencies, who may not all have the same level of understanding with regard to protection and the need for good policies. So, even if the social services department concerned has a good standard of policies and awareness of their importance, the service they purchase on behalf of a person with learning disabilities may not. So Plyedale Social Services Department may have a Policy for the Protection of Vulnerable Adults but Librecare, an independent organisation providing residential care, hasn't got round to it. Plydale Social Services Department then has a responsibility, as a potential purchaser of Librecare's services, to ask questions about the existence of such a policy and their attitude towards safeguarding people who are vulnerable. If the answer is 'Yes, a policy exists', then Plydale could ask to read the document, check that it's active and that staff receive regular training in how it works. If the answer is 'No', it would be interesting to see if the very question itself is spur enough to get Librecare going. If not, it would also be interesting to see if Plydale considers looking elsewhere for the service required. The issue of commissioning is covered in the *No Secrets* document.

Having policies is the first step. Staff training is the next. It's no good having a policy and guidelines, if staff don't know of their existence nor how they affect them in their daily work environments. And staff change – they move on or up – so training should be a rolling programme, that is adaptable by being able to incorporate new insights, new understanding of practice. These can be built into the recruitment and induction processes and the ongoing training of all staff. We say more about this in the next chapter.

> '*The things we were arguing for 15 years ago are now beginning to happen . . . things like police references (regarding the sex offenders register), circles of support, risk assessment on activities.*'
>
> *Dino*

Parents

Parents can and should be supported in their protective role, although not all courses of action will be appropriate or possible for everyone. It's a case of knowing what can be done, and going for what is most manageable for you. Knowing, accepting and understanding how and why people with learning disabilities are vulnerable to abuse/Abuse is the first key step – acknowledging the fears that you have kept deep inside, examining them and bringing them down to a size you can deal with. This is such a hard subject and causes degrees of pain and anxiety with all the parents we have worked with.

The second step is action: what can the parent do to minimise risk and maximise safety? It was from one particular parents' group that the idea of a Protection Portfolio developed. The discussion turned to the number of different care givers involved in their children's lives, when one parent burst out in some anguish with the question, 'How can I trust anyone?' This led the group to think about what they actually could do to take some control of their child's vulnerability, and the Protection Portfolio grew from that.

Essentially, the Protection Portfolio is a collection of facts and information about a vulnerable child, or young person, brought together in a positive way for the purpose of showing that the child is loved and protected within their own family and circle of care. The information/details are written down and put in a ring binder file which is attractively decorated and presented. Also included is a statement that the parents or carers of the person concerned have received training and learned about how and why sexual abuse happens and what they might do to prevent it. The idea is that parents show the Protection Portfolio to anyone with any caring or supervisory responsibility for their child, especially those who provide physical care and/or are ever alone with their child. Everyone is included, from taxi drivers, child sitters, teachers, care staff and relatives. There are two reasons for showing the Protection Portfolio – first, to try to draw in others positively as co-protectors of their child, and, secondly, to deter anybody who may be set on abusing their child. To date, only a small number of parents have gone through the necessary training, prepared their own portfolios and started showing them. But the results so far lead us to believe that there is huge potential in this idea because, at the very least, it affirms parents in their protecting role. And, at the most, it both strengthens the protective circle around the person and deters potential abusers.

It is also well worth reading *Proud Child, Safer Child* by Merry Cross, which we mentioned earlier. Specifically written for parents and carers, it sets out to provide them with the information and skills they need to protect their children. It's full of information and practical suggestions for what can be done. A second recommended publication is *The Day We Found Her Crying*, by Deborah Kitson and Jane Livingstone. This helps and advises parents of adults with learning disabilities on how to respond to the sexual abuse of their son or daughter, and, more importantly, suggests ideas for preventing it happening in the first place.

Another very practical way forward is via 'protective behaviours'. This is a relatively new approach in the UK and has much to commend it in relation to disabled children and adults, although its use does require some reasoning, reflection, a degree of abstract thought and verbal communication. The protective behaviours approach has two themes – first, that we all have the right to feel safe all the time, and, secondly, that there is nothing so awful we can't talk about it with someone. With appropriate guidance, individuals begin by finding out about the difference within them between situations where they feel safe, are having fun, feel scared in an adventurous situation, the feelings where a risk is being taken on purpose, and those feelings experienced when unsafe. Within each one of us, and unique to us, is an early warning sign, when our body begins to let us know that we are feeling unsafe. Going on the big dipper can be easy for one, thrilling for another and terrifying for a third. Our bodies let us know what we feel. Having helped the person identify his or her early warning feeling, the protective behaviours approach then goes on to suggest ways in which that person can respond to them by seeking the help they need from a person they have previously identified as being safe and trustworthy.

Parents can feel very alone in their fears. From our group work with parents we have seen terrific benefits in the way mutual support has been offered from a base of shared under-standing and sympathy. Many parents have said to us that no one else quite knows what it's like to be a parent of a child or adult with learning disabilities, except another person in the same situation. This doesn't mean all parents think the same or have parallel experiences, they too are all individuals. But there is usually enough common ground between them, when they discuss how each is personally affected by the reality of disabil-ity, for the group-work approach to be a productive way of working with parents. If you are part of a parents' group, that group might consider inviting someone well versed on this issue to help you with some training and/or awareness raising to meet the particular needs of the group members.

Protective communities

These include all known people in the child's life and those who she/he may briefly encounter who are otherwise not known. Beyond the really familiar people, such as family members, school staff, workers in social services and volunteers for instance, other people also have protecting opportunities. For example, neighbours, people in the street, at church, in shops etc. But we know from a number of 'child abuse cases' in the media how difficult it can be for individuals, especially if the child is not known to them, to act appropriately when a child is under threat or even to be able to recognise the threat. As we discussed earlier, ordinary people such as ourselves, members of communities, have to accept first that disabled children actually are at risk. Secondly, we need to consider whether we would be prepared to act should we suspect something untoward. Thirdly, it would help to know what we might do in such a situation, so we need to get informed about the options. One small-scale example of an 'aware' community is that of a local church in our area, which has just completed a child protection policy with accompanying guidelines for the young people who are part of the congregation. Apart from the value of having a protecting document, the process of informing and consulting people has been very helpful in widening their understanding of the subject and appreciation of what steps they can take to protect all the young people they may encounter. We have heard about an approach called circles of support, promoted in the UK by an organisation called Circles Network. This is a national voluntary organisation with an educational objective to build inclusive communities. The aim is to support socially excluded or isolated people to become included in community life. Circles Network assists people to develop circles of support, and build networks of friends who agree to support them in a non-patronising, non-judgemental way to achieve their dreams. The families project is an example of their work; here, parents who have learning disabilities, and want to parent their children effectively, are helped to do so.

The protective environments of some children and adults with learning disabilities are likely to be fragile for some of the reasons discussed earlier, a key one being that disabled people are seen as of lesser value. Merry Cross quotes a director of social services who, after giving a talk about his department's child protection policy, was asked about disabled children. He said, 'Let me deal with the normal children first'. That sort of belief shows how far we have to go in effectively keeping disabled children as safe as possible. Yet that director, as an individual and in his professional role, is part of each disabled child's protective environment.

The person with learning disabilities
We have said that the degree to which each person is truly able to take some responsibility for self-protection depends upon a number of individual and other factors which all play their own

distinctive part. There is a fine balancing act to manage between an individual's rights and capacity to manage the consequences of those rights and parents' natural response to protect. However, this natural response can have the opposite effect by risking greater danger. An example is Catherine, aged 38.

Catherine

Her parents refused all the efforts of the day centre staff to allow her to take part in a healthy living course, because they saw it as 'sexualising' her. Certain that Catherine was not at all interested 'in anything like that' they thought they were protecting her by excluding her from it. The fact that she was in a day centre and mixing, often unsupervised, with other users, some of whom did exhibit highly sexualised behaviour, meant she was not 'safe' from sexual contact, whether she was interested or not.

She may not necessarily participate in anything, but is likely at least to observe the behaviour of others.

The best way forward is to think about how to equip people with the personal and practical skills by which they can appropriately be expected to take some responsibility for protecting themselves. And to the degree that this is beyond the ability of the person to do so, then parents, carers, workers and others will protect and safeguard as part of their respective responsibilities outlined above.

STRATEGIES FOR WORKING TOWARDS THE PERSONAL SAFETY OF PEOPLE WITH LEARNING DISABILITIES

Sexuality work

We deliberately use this phrase rather than 'sex education' because 'sexuality' has wider implications, as we saw at the beginning of this book. We are not just talking about the 'facts of life', although many people with learning disabilities do need to have such information. (Some, however, do not: it would be inappropriate for them to know about sexual intercourse, although entirely appropriate to them to know that masturbation is OK. Deciding what is appropriate or not for each individual may not be that easy. Although it may be clear that an individual is unlikely to have and sustain a sexual relationship, they may have bits of information or misinformation about sex that needs to be clarified.) Here, we mean something much broader. All of us need to know about our bodies and how they work, how to get on with other people and act responsibly towards them and ourselves. For those who do embark on sexual relationships, there can only be benefits from having accurate information and feeling confident in managing these relationships. What needs to be learned depends largely upon the person's disability and also on his or her age. What is taught to an able 12-year-old will be more than (or at least different from) a woman of 30 who has severe learning disabilities. The purpose of good quality sexuality work is to give appropriate information, build self-esteem and confidence, develop and practise social skills alongside an understanding of their purpose and knowledge/techniques for keeping safe and healthy. What a sexuality programme actually comprises will vary according to whether the participants are at the moderate end of the spectrum or more severely disabled. It will certainly need to be tailored to the needs of each individual. We look at this in detail in the next chapter. But the point we are making is that virtually all people with learning disabilities can participate in and benefit from sexuality work. In terms of vulnerability and keeping safe, they need to acquire a good sense of self and a basic grasp of sexuality issues, such as knowing which parts of the body are private, so that they can understand, for example, acceptable or unacceptable behaviour, safe or unsafe touch, and so what is or is not abusive.

Self-esteem
This means enabling people with learning disabilities to feel good about who they are and about being themselves. To some extent it's an uphill task, because of the way society views learning disability. Poor self-image and vulnerability feed off each other. If people 'know' that they are of less value to others or experience being 'put down', they may feel that anything abusive is somehow deserved or that they are not worth protecting. Valerie Sinason, a consultant child psychotherapist, who works with sexually abused people with learning disabilities writes about the 'guilt' a child who has learning disabilities

experiences. 'He feels he should not have been born and that people wish he were dead.' Such a feeling, remaining unexplored and unhealed, will result in a very low sense of personal value. Where this is very deep in an individual, then very skilled professional help is needed. However, for other people, it is possible to work in a way that does encourage them, boosts their confidence and helps them to see that they do matter. There is a crucial role here for parents, carers, family members and workers who will need self-consciously to work towards building self-esteem, even though society 'out there' sometimes seems to be moving in the opposite direction. You may have come across People First, which is a self-advocacy group run by and for people with learning disabilities.

Communication

By communication we mean the giving and receiving of messages or signals, not necessarily verbal, that have a meaning. Good communication 'is a large and vital part of the protective cloak we need to place around' a child with learning disabilities (Merry Cross). So it's about knowing and understanding the individual's particular communication method and using it respectfully. Respect is very important, because it says to them that you are willing to go with their system, rather than expecting them to use yours, which may not be possible for them. We also need to remember that even if someone has good verbal communication, they may not be able to tell anyone if they are being abused. This may be due to a lack of understanding about what is happening, not having the right words to explain it, or for all the other reasons that people don't tell, such as fear. For a person who uses alternative communication methods, for example, British Sign Language, Makaton or Blissboard, where possible, it is helpful if a vocabulary could be given that would indicate all is not well. Where such a vocabulary cannot be given, carers need to be alert to other non-verbal signs, such as changes in behaviour or emotional distress.

Personal and intimate care

This is an area which offers considerable opportunity for abuse. The person with a learning disability is in a very dependent situation with someone else having access to the most private parts of his or her body. For many people with learning disabilities intimate care is a fundamental part of their daily routine, because of the nature of their disability, and has been so from the minute they were born. It can be really hard for a parent, or carer, to get this right. Take toilet training as an example. Such programmes cannot help but have a fundamental and lasting effect on the growing sexuality and self-esteem of the person concerned. If not done sensitively, with care for the person's right to privacy and respect for his or her own body, a programme can desensitise the person to being touched around the genital area by other people. This will have profound consequences in terms of vulnerability. So, if such people have not experienced anything other, they may be unable to judge whether what happens, how it is done and who does it are right or wrong, good or bad. However, there is a level at which the person knows if they are comfortable or not, whether they feel safe or not. In recognising this enormous degree of vulnerability and risk, what can be done? We talked earlier about policies and procedures and staff training in awareness and good practice. This is about creating good structures that seek to protect, and then working within them in ways that ensure dignity and respect. So intimate care needs to be provided in the best possible way, with the support of a quality policy. And the person with learning disabilities should be involved during the intimate care routine in ways that help them to be less passive. Examples of good practice would be:

- Letting the person make choices, such as about which soap to use and what piece of underwear to put on
- Aiming for maximum privacy by keeping the person covered up as much as possible whilst the personal care is being provided
- Involving the person as much as possible in the process; for example, giving them a soaped flannel to wash whatever parts they can manage
- Most certainly, where adults with learning disabilities are concerned, ensure that it is a female worker who provides the care to a woman and vice versa for males. This is particularly important in a care rather than a nursing setting. In a clinical environment it seems reasonably acceptable to have intimate procedures done by someone of the opposite gender, although many people, especially women, definitely prefer to have a

female nurse. This preference should be respected as far as possible. Care settings are different in a number of ways. The environment is likely to be a significant and continuing part of the life of the person with learning disabilities. Care workers are less likely to be professionally qualified in the way that clinicians are, who have their own particular training, code of practice and registration procedures. So the practice of care workers may be less tightly regulated and prescribed (although the majority would seek to work in a professional manner). It is important that the service or organisation in which such care is provided does all it can to ensure maximum respect and safety, by reducing all opportunities for potential abusers to target vulnerable people and one way of doing this is to ensure same gender care.

- Parents or staff bathing a boy may notice an erection. This may be because of a need to urinate or simply be a spontaneous event that is a normal part of being male. If responded to in a calm and respectful way the person receives good messages about their sexuality and that it isn't a problem.
- Consistency in the way intimate care is carried out is also important. Those who provide it need to agree on what is the preferred procedure and maintain that.

Empowering

By this we mean encouraging people with learning disabilities to have meaningful choices and, with appropriate support, to be able to make decisions that affect their lives. Ideally this needs doing from the earliest days in childhood so that it becomes a natural way of life rather than 'added on' sometime in adulthood. If small and appropriate choices are made all the time about the most mundane things – for example, what to have for breakfast – then the foundations are laid, whereby individuals can learn to do the same about their bodies. They need to be able to say 'no' to something they don't feel safe with, and have that respected. Equally, empowerment may mean the person is encouraged to say 'yes' which is fine, as long as it is safe and appropriate for that person. How 'appropriate' is determined is the all-important question and must be determined, as we have said elsewhere, in the context of each individual's life. However, the main point is: if there aren't the opportunities to make decisions and choices over little things, then there is little skill or confidence in making a choice about a big thing.

Vulnerability is a key component in how and why certain people are abused and we have also said that vulnerability is often a significant feature of the life of a person with learning disabilities. However, the more that measures such as those above are put into place, the better protected the person is likely to be.

The relevance of language

Language has a key role in either affirming someone and doing them down. Language is powerful because it not only reflects, but reinforces, the way we think about things. So, being sensitive to the words that are used does matter. For example, a number of disability-related words and phrases have been absorbed into playground terminology and used in ways designed to insult or hurt. Words such as idiot, Mongol and moron have been around for a long while. Others are spassy (spastic), or crip (crippled). In the 1970s, Joey Deacon become a household name when his life story was published and then televised. In it he detailed his struggles as a disabled person growing up in institutional care. This story was a strong affirmation of the power of the human spirit. And yet a taunt developed soon afterwards which targeted 'different' children (those who were recognisably disabled) as 'Deeks'.

Greater sensitivity is gradually being shown, however. Think of the changes from 'deaf aid' to hearing aid; 'blind dog' to guide dog, and the letting go of 'mentally handicapped' in preference to learning difficulty/learning disability. All this may seem pointless, but these things matter greatly to the people they concern. Terminology, in reflecting our wider attitudes, is greatly influential in whether we knock down or build up the sense of self-worth of the people we are referring to. It is all too easy to do the former by thoughtlessness and a little care will achieve the latter. Parents of children with learning disabilities can also get caught up in this, by professionals casting them as 'difficult' or 'unco-operative' when, in fact, they may just be trying to get themselves and their views heard. It is important that great care and sensitivity are shown when choosing words so that no one is diminished by such thoughtlessness.

'If we don't protect, who will?'

Dino

There are questions parents could ask of professionals and agencies in respect of protection:

• How safe will my son or daughter be in your service?
• What steps have you taken to make her/him as safe as possible?
• If something were to happen, what response will you make?
• How will you keep me informed on all this?

8 Dealing with the realities: sexuality work

We've talked much about the reality of sexuality and vulnerability within the lives of people with learning disabilities and how it's impossible to ignore either. We wonder how you're feeling at this stage in the book; the likelihood is that you've gone through a whole range of emotions, depending on your particular situation and your son or daughter's abilities, how pessimistic or optimistic you feel about the subject, and how it relates to her/him. We've tried to approach sexuality and vulnerability as separate issues, but as you see they can't be kept apart for long. When we do workshops on sexuality, vulnerability is a key component; when we do workshops on vulnerability, then sexuality has to be included. They may seem completely unrelated to each other, but in fact they are not. One way of looking at their relationship is to describe each as being one side of the same coin: apparently facing in opposite directions yet part of each other. In this chapter we talk about what should be done with this 'coin', and the best response: sexuality work. Just as we said in the introduction that sexuality is about much more than the physical aspects of our bodies concerned with sexual activity and reproduction, so sex education/sexuality work needs to be regarded in the same broad way.

One way of looking at this is to say that learning about sexuality

is not an isolated topic but is part of the wider themes of relationships, health and safety, moral responsibility and self-esteem. It encourages the development of positive attitudes and values such as care for others, responsibility for self and others, tolerance and consideration. It fosters the development of skills such as assertiveness, decision making and communication.

This definition doesn't specifically mention education on sex. This isn't because the 'S' word is being deliberately avoided, but rather that a much wider definition is needed, and not only for children and adults with learning disabilities. The term 'sexuality work' itself may be unsatisfactory to some people. Their view is that any mention of 'sex' or 'sexuality' is too limiting, and may put off some parents who otherwise might consider their child taking part in some of this learning. The contrary view is that unless either of these words is mentioned in the title, a charge of being misleading could be reasonably made. Perhaps a good way forward is to describe the work in some such way as 'building blocks for life' or 'healthy living', with a subtitle that incorporates 'sex' and/or 'sexuality' in an appropriate way. However that is resolved, the definition above is good, because it has a sense of inclusiveness: that is, that *all* people can benefit from sexuality work, with the proviso that what is taught must be carefully tailored to the needs, requirements and learning styles of each individual participant. This is absolutely essential and is woven into everything we say in this chapter. Before we go on to examine what ingredients are essential to a good sexuality course, it may be helpful to take time to set the scene.

RE-ACTIVE AND PRO-ACTIVE RESPONSES

Although sexuality work (in the formal education sense) is being done with some children and adults with learning disabilities within many schools, day centres, other service localities and within families there is a risk, for various reasons, of it being done in a piecemeal fashion. By this we mean that some information is given for perhaps a few weeks or months only and then stops. This unconnected situation has been and still is the case for children and young people without learning disabilities, so there is still some distance to go within the whole topic generally. Having said that, with regard to people with learning disabilities, there has been definite progress over the past three decades in recognising the need for work to be done and in the range of resources available for devising and running courses. But much more remains to be done to highlight the absolute importance of this subject, devise ways of making sure no one is left out for any reason and provide quality learning opportunities.

At present much of the work that is done tends to be *re-active*: that means, responding to an existing need or pressing problem. For example:

Nina

A mother, whose daughter Nina is 12 and attends a special school for children with moderate learning disabilities, contacted us for help and advice. Nina is approaching puberty and has a poor idea of good personal hygiene. Her mother wanted to know what she could do. We felt that the school was the obvious place to provide this learning, and her mother was willing to support it at home. On contacting the school we were told that sex education was planned for Nina in the next school year.

Ian

Ian enjoys evenings at his local leisure club for people with learning disabilities; it's a chance to meet different people. Pete is a new volunteer to the club. During Pete's first evening there, Ian introduces him to Gloria, saying that she is his girlfriend – within seconds they are all over each other. Later in the evening Pete sees Ian smooching with Annie, equally closely, whilst Gloria is similarly engaged with someone else. Pete senses confusion and a lack of understanding within the club members about what a girl or boyfriend is and also within the workers and volunteers about what to do.

Parvez and George

Parvez and George are 16 and 17. They make a beeline for each other whenever they meet up at the Sycamores, which provides short-break care. Staff are very concerned and don't know what to do as Parvez and George head for a quiet place. Some suggest talking it through with the parents; others suggest simply re-arranging the bookings so that they don't meet.

These situations illustrate simply some everyday examples of people with learning disabilities who may not yet know enough to keep safe, behave appropriately and feel good about themselves and their bodies. Each situation also presents a good starting point for sexuality work to be considered. What appears to be a crisis can be turned into an opportunity. Unfortunately, work in response to specific problems may only offer short-term solutions. Rather than risk questions, such as 'How can we meet this person's needs?', it becomes 'How do we manage this person's behaviour?' Short-term or re-active interventions usually do not go to the heart of the problem, but are chosen because the more appropriate ones demand long-term commitment and may seem too hard.

The *pro-active* approach is where work starts almost from birth and continues throughout life, anticipating needs before they arise, thus lessening the possibility of a crisis occurring later on. If parents can become self-consciously aware of their role in this area and from the earliest days, then this will have a great impact on the life of their son or daughter who has learning disabilities. By putting the whole subject of sexuality to the centre of the stage, parents and other key people are able to start preparing the child, and themselves, for their life as a sexual being. At present very little of this is being done. Our hope is that in, say, two generations from now, far fewer people with learning disabilities (and their carers) will be facing the sort of problems that are all too common today.

THE NEED FOR WORK TO BE DONE

The fundamental aim of sexuality work is to empower people with learning disabilities, by giving them appropriate (to each individual) knowledge and information about sexuality and by enhancing self-esteem. 'Sexuality work must be based on self-esteem work if it is going to achieve its purpose' (Dino).

For some people with damaged self-esteem, good work done well will go some way to repairing that damage. We cannot overestimate the importance of this 'purpose' that Dino refers to. For example, we hear of vulnerable, isolated women who have mild or moderate learning disabilities, who are targeted by unscrupulous men, with the sole intention of sexually exploiting them, or of abusing their children. Giving them, and all people with learning disabilities, the tools they need to protect themselves or be protected, will go some way to reducing vulnerability. There still is a reticence about looking sexuality in the face, when it comes to people with learning disabilities. Until we do, there will be untold consequences for future generations.

More and more parents and workers are seeing a need for sexuality work to be done, and one purpose of this book is to put forward a strong case for that. The difficulty is in knowing how to go about it and who should do it. Many parents are naturally concerned about this because they know that if it goes wrong or backfires, they will have to cope with the consequences as will their son or daughter. Generally speaking, we believe that professionals such as teachers, social workers, day centre workers, support assistants, health workers, advocacy workers, school nurses etc are, potentially, with good training, preparation and support, in a good position to provide sexuality work. Many will not want to be sexuality educators though. No one should feel pressurised into doing it. But, whoever does do it, parents are crucial in ensuring the learning is supported and applied in all relevant aspects of their child's life. If a parent wants to do sexuality 'teaching', then that would also be good and would certainly be strengthened if school, and/or other service providers, are backing it up formally and informally to ensure consistency of information and approach.

PARENTS AS SEXUALITY EDUCATORS

In this section we are talking about the organised, self-conscious teaching that parents might decide to take on for themselves. What it is they teach depends entirely on the age of the child/ young person, the nature and level of disability and what it is they need to know. A clear example is a mother deciding how she is to prepare her daughter for the start of menstruation. How much the child is able to understand and what responsibility she can or cannot take for managing this will determine just how much information is given. If the child has a severe learning disability it will probably not be appropriate to explain about fallopian tubes and how the menstrual cycle works, for example. Understanding that the bleeding is normal, how to fix pads, when to change them and where to dispose of them may be enough – and a significant achievement in itself. 'I have given up on tampons and returned to pads in order to be able to demonstrate to Kate what they're for and how to use them' (Lizzie).

A father may take it upon himself to help his son feel OK about erections and wet dreams, that it's normal and even something to be proud of. A parent might share a behaviour programme with school which teaches the child or young person about public and private activities, and places to ensure that masturbation, for example, is done consistently in an agreed private place such as the bedroom.

Every day is likely to provide many opportunities for talking and educating about issues such as:

- The physical differences between males and females and the reason for them. Here is a chance to use the 'proper' words if that's appropriate, or words that the young person is most likely to understand, for private parts of the body, and doing so in a way that enables the child to feel good about themselves. This may be really embarrassing at first but, believe us, it does get easier with practice!

- Which person or people have the right to see the child's unclothed body and in what circumstances, and, by definition, who does not have that right. Similarly making clear who can touch the child's body and exactly which parts. This is very important for children and adults who need help with personal and intimate care, because they can get all too used to many different people having legitimate access to their most private areas, thereby losing that natural sense of self-privacy and be particularly vulnerable.

- Periods and wet dreams are, as mentioned above, excellent opportunities for parents to help the young person understand what is going on and to feel OK about it.

- Masturbation will certainly need responding to if it occurs in inappropriate places as it may well do. Here, too, is a chance to give a positive message, to male and female alike, that this is normal, but is an activity that should only be carried out at certain times and in certain places. Parents rarely get involved in this area of their non-disabled child's life once adolescence has been reached, because the child/young person has by this time developed a natural sense of what is appropriate and what isn't.

- Love and sex (sexual relationships, marriage, intercourse, contraception, pregnancy) – whether information is given about any of these, or indeed how much, will depend on the individual person, and, most especially, on the level of their disability and the degree to which these issues are likely to be a part of their life. Careful judgement will be needed as well as honesty with oneself about whose needs are being met if the decision is taken *not* to give the information. For example, Mrs D doesn't tell her daughter Anya about contraception because she fears it will encourage her to have sex. However, Anya is already engaging in secret 'heavy petting' sessions with a young man at her day centre and he also knows nothing of contraception.

The fact of a parent feeling that their son or daughter is unlikely to marry is not, in itself, a good enough reason for that person not to receive information about sexual relationships. Knowledge about such things is, for many people, like a passport to the adult world. There will be many people with learning disabilities who do need to understand about these things, even though they may never go on to practise them.

PROFESSIONALS AS SEXUALITY EDUCATORS

It is encouraging when parents take on the task of educating their children about sexuality matters; even better when it is a shared task between parent and professional/worker. It's important to state that parents shouldn't feel they have to take on this formal educating role. For perfectly good reasons, many parents choose to maintain a low profile in this area, which is absolutely fine. The reality is, though, that it's more likely to be a professional who takes on this role. Certainly in school, and secondary schools especially, some sex education will be done by a teacher. However, if the young person who has a learning disability is in a mainstream school, the chances are that little concession will be made to their particular requirements in terms of what they need to know and how it should be taught. Sex education also takes place in special schools, but there is an enormous variation in what is taught, how, and to whom. Also schools are incredibly busy places and much depends on whether any member of staff is comfortable with the subject and willing to do it to a sufficiently high standard. For adults with learning disabilities access to good quality sexuality work is a random affair. It is most likely to take place in day services and usually given only to people who have been identified as being in need, because of their behaviours or obvious vulnerabilities.

We are aware that there are people outside the learning disability services who appear to function reasonably well. They are likely to miss out on any work to do with sexuality, because they appear to be so able, yet their needs for information and to be safe are likely to be particularly acute, because their seeming ability masks their gaps and vulnerabilities.

When workers are considering doing sexuality work with children, young people or adults care should be taken to address the following issues:

What is taught must be only what that person needs to know

This point is not about withholding information; as we have said before, people with learning disabilities would have the same right to know as the rest of us. However, too much information or information that is beyond a person's capacity to deal with is risky for them. (We may all know how to switch on our central heating, and maybe even how to programme the times, but to expect us to service the gas boiler ourselves would, in most cases, be asking for trouble.) Clearly, there is also a right and a wrong time for particular pieces of information and knowledge to be given; for any one individual person, what is taught at 15 will be different to what they would have been taught at ten, and at 25 would be different to 15. It will all depend on the person's life, circumstances, disability and the need to know.

The learning must be done very slowly

This may mean spending many weeks or months on one particular aspect, and returning to it again and again, in order to weave it into the whole complex picture. Most of us learn over a period of time, rather than just by hearing something once and immediately knowing it. That is even truer of people with learning impairments whose individual and particular learning requirements must be understood first. So a subject such as masturbation or keeping safe would not be dealt with in a single session and then closed. What is taught should be reiterated, reinterpreted and reshaped – in a spiral fashion – as the work progresses. This all takes time. Let's look at Darren's situation.

Darren

Darren is 26 and goes to a day centre where he exhibits some unacceptable sexual behaviour, mostly touching the breasts of other service users and also some of the staff. Guidelines are drawn up to deal with the behaviour as it is now, and at the same time one of the male workers begins a programme of sexuality work with him. This is made more difficult because Darren's parents don't want to know; they deny that there is any problem. So rather than diving in quickly to try to deal with the things Darren needs to know, the worker spends four months (seeing him once a week) simply building trust and being consistent. This is because the worker recognises that little progress will be made with Darren, and in fact may make matters worse, if good groundwork is not done first. When the worker is confident that has been achieved his plan is to move on, but still very slowly. After six months the worker's manager begins to question the level of input going to one person when there are another 70 people who attend the day centre. So although it is recognised that work should be done to the best possible standard, other issues have now come to the fore which threaten that.

What should be learnt from this situation? Staff/colleagues and managers especially need to understand all that's involved within this subject and be willing and able to support it as far as possible. In Darren's case, pressure on resources such as staff time may mean the work stops before it truly begins. If that's so, Darren is left with the practical and emotional consequences of having his learning and behavioural needs unmet, and those who work with him will continue to struggle. In an ideal world the worker would continue to see Darren for years, reassessing as time passes what his learning needs are and devising ways of meeting them. Our world is not ideal though, so there is always a tension between what should be regarded as best possible practice and what realistically can be done in as good and safe a way as possible. In the next chapter, we talk about what agencies can and should do in situations like that of Darren.

WORKER/EDUCATOR TRAINING

Professionals planning to embark on doing sexuality work need to be well prepared. The following questions need to be asked of (and by) the workers who are planning to be involved in this:
- How comfortable are they in doing this sensitive work?
- What is their value base regarding people with learning disabilities?

- What is their understanding of how sexuality fits into the way in which people with learning disabilities are devalued and oppressed?
- Are they coming to the work from a particular moral standpoint? It's impossible to be morally neutral in this work, so it does matter that potential workers are helped to be aware of their position. This is likely to be especially important to parents. For example, what are their views on casual sexual encounters, sex before marriage, on homosexual relationships, on abortion? Also of importance, are they sensitive to the views of other people which are different from their own?

Preparation of the workplace
This is discussed in the next chapter.

Preparing to work with parents and carers
We have said that parents and carers often come across as being 'over-protective', which may in effect be hiding an intuitive understanding of their son or daughter's 'gaps'. Therefore, workers need to be listening to and hearing what parents and carers have to say, and in Chapter 5 we discussed how workers could go about it. The unique and special knowledge of parents is crucial to the planning and carrying out of the work and how it's implemented in real life.

> *'Parents must be involved: although not in the sessions themselves, they need to know what's happening. Parents carry the responsibility. Whatever goes wrong, the child comes back to you at the end of the day.'*
>
> *Theresa*

Some parents will not want work to be done, or will believe it's not necessary, which may conflict with the wishes of their (adult or nearly adult) son or daughter. Whilst parents have the right to decide what is best in terms of their children when under age, that is 18, once they reach adulthood they too have the right to an opinion regarding their sexuality, their lives and access to learning. If the parent and adult (or nearly adult) person disagree, one way forward is to seek an advocate for both, and certainly for the person with learning disabilities who has least power of all. The advocate could be a social worker, someone from an advocacy service, a member of People First, for example. If the person lives permanently away from their parents, those parents' rights are likely to have lessened, unless they are consistently key people in their daughter or son's life and of course many parents still are.

Preparing to do the work

The following questions and points need to be considered:

- Is the worker aware of the support network of the person who has the learning disability? This, in essence, means the family (you), or, if the person is an adult and has moved away from their parents, those who are involved in their housing and caring environment.
- Do the workers know those in the network, and is the support network aware of the proposed course, and what is to be taught? Have they been consulted as appropriate and involved in the planning?

Quite often the families/carers are not consulted and this is because those delivering the work have not always clarified in their own minds what is the parents/carers' role and place. Their role is vital in supporting the learning, encouraging the person with learning disabilities as they apply it in real life, and in ensuring that it takes root.

Doing the work

There are some important questions that need to be asked. For example, do the workers have proper knowledge of the person's learning disability and how it affects their learning? Will the teaching methods be sufficiently varied and flexible to take account of those particular learning difficulties?

Eve, who cares for her sister Debbie aged 30, asks: 'If someone isn't able to learn through the way that you teach, have you (that is, the worker) the knowledge and resources to teach in a way that they can learn?'

We all learn in different ways, according to how our brains are organised, which is also true of people with learning disabilities. However, the cognitive impairment or damage to the brain in a person with learning disabilities is an additional factor and needs acknowledging. This can be hard for some workers who, in a respectful attempt to avoid defining a person solely by their disability, see it as a problem of attitude on the part of society. However, this may prohibit the worker taking a more realistic position, where the learning disability or cognitive impairment has to be acknowledged in order for the whole person to be seen.

- How can workers be sure the information given has been understood, and what ways or methods are being set up to check on this?

Evaluating the effectiveness of sexuality work in people with a learning disability is not easy, but does need to be done. A worker told us the following story of a time, many years ago, when he worked in a day centre.

Gary and Sally

Gary and Sally, two of the day centre users, were planning marriage, and had the support of their families. The worker who talked to us did some work with them on contraception, particularly about condoms: how they work and how they should be put on. He decided to use the top part of a broom handle as a prop for the condom teaching. All seemed to go well and be understood. Six months later and with some anxiety, Sally came to him and said she thought she might be pregnant. When the worker checked with Gary about their use of condoms, Gary was puzzled about Sally possibly being pregnant. He reassured the worker that they took the broomstick plus condom to bed with them each night.

- Linked with the point just made, it's important therefore to check whether the worker really appreciates the place of acquiescence in the lives of people with learning disabilities. This is where people say 'yes' when really meaning 'no' because that's what they think is required of them, thus appearing to give consent, or to understand, but in fact not doing so. Acquiescence can place people with learning disabilities in particularly vulnerable positions. One consequence, therefore is that the worker receives feedback from the person with learning disabilities which gives the impression that the teaching is going in when in fact it isn't at all. As Dino points out: 'Professionals . . . often don't understand the level of compliance and acquiescence that many people with learning

disabilities exhibit. Parents also get the blame for this; it's as though our sons and daughters are vulnerable because we can't let go.'
- Support and supervision for the educators. Who will provide it, when and how often?

It's very important that workers receive regular supervision in order to achieve good standards of practice and also to be accountable for what they are doing.
- After the course has finished, will the worker still be around to offer support if it's needed?

As Eve comments: 'Sexuality workers are in powerful positions because of the effect they can have on people's lives, yet they may not fully understand or witness those effects.' She expresses a fear of many parents that is tied up with acquiescence: 'The saying "yes" may easily be the thing the learning disabled person learns, without the complicated self-protective process being learnt of saying "no".'

As we've argued earlier in this book, professionals have the duty and responsibility to take that further step in building a purposeful relationship with parents over the issue of sexuality education. Parents may feel that workers do not properly understand the gaps in the ability of their son or daughter which may lead to problems later. For example, a key objective of sexuality work is to build self-esteem which is good in itself and also aids learning. If workers are not fully aware of the cognitive and learning gaps, it is likely that information may be given inappropriately. So the message of empowerment is given and received, but if inappropriate information is given or correct information given in inappropriate ways, the person may be unable to retain and use this when it's needed. A situation may arise then, when the person remembers that they have rights and power and feels good about that but, if not able to hold on to important information (say about ways of keeping safe), may find him or herself more vulnerable than before the work began. This is a key issue for parents who may intuitively sense the ways in which their son or daughter is vulnerable if proper care isn't taken by workers to really get to know the person's needs before work starts, and be prepared to adjust and adapt the content of the course as it proceeds and the worker's understanding increases.

Compatibility of group members

If work is to be delivered to a group of people, it is important for there to be a level of compatibility amongst its members, for example, in terms of intellectual ability, life experience and emotional health, so that the learning needs of individuals are not too diverse to meet effectively. So if one member is far more able than others, the workers may have to pitch the learning at a level too low for her, leaving her bored or frustrated. Similarly, the person whose learning ability is less than the rest, may flounder whilst their needs are being met.

A SAMPLE SEXUALITY PROGRAMME

Amy

Amy has profound learning disabilities. Her programme is likely to cover something on making choices, knowing she's a young woman, feeling good about herself, being part of a family and feeling safe.

Indira

Indira has a severe learning disability. In addition to the above, she will probably learn about private parts of the body, keeping healthy (diet, personal cleanliness and hygiene during menstruation), gender differences, socially appropriate behaviour, keeping safe, possibly sexual activity such as masturbation, the needs of other people, friendships and putting right any misinformation.

Harry

Harry has a very mild learning disability. He needs to know about all the above, as well as girlfriends and boyfriends, sexual relationships including sexual intercourse, contraception especially condoms, safer sex and sexually transmitted infections, marriage and possibly parenthood and its realities, sexual vulnerabilities, respecting women and having any misinformation put right.

These are just suggestions. Remember: what is taught is what the person needs to know, no more, no less than that. And what they need to know depends on such variable factors as level of the disability, age and circumstances of the person concerned.

We would also like to suggest three different models of devising and running a programme. These are:

- a programme planned in advance which is followed through session by session.

- an ecological method, which has clear aims but how these are met is a collaborative effort between workers and participants, and is shaped as time passes and the needs of the participants gradually emerge.

- a modular approach where distinct parts of a programme are delivered within definite timescales such as a school or college term.

Planning and carrying out the work must take into account the points made earlier in this chapter. We are aware of a number of training courses throughout the country for workers planning to deliver sexuality programmes, some of which are accredited. We ourselves are developing a course, which will also respond to the need for good quality training in this crucial area, hoping that it too can be part of an accreditation system.

It's worth restating that sexuality work, done well, has the potential for raising self-esteem in a person and therefore their quality of life. It isn't necessarily the role of an expert: as we've said, all people involved in the life of a person with learning disabilities have, to a greater or lesser extent, an educating role whether or not they realise it. It is now time to ensure this is done well, appropriately and consistently.

9 Implications for service agencies

We refer here to the whole wide range of statutory and non-statutory bodies involved in providing a service to people with learning disabilities from the early years of life onwards. The big organisations are social services departments, education and services provided by health trusts. Health services range from clinical interventions, by GPs, nurses and hospitals, for example, to social/community resources, such as staffed group homes for adults with learning disabilities previously living in long-stay institutions. Health and social services also work together on planning service provision within their shared areas as a way of making the most of limited resources and encourage a better working together. If you are in touch with a community team for learning disabilities (or similar title), it is likely to comprise social workers from social services and community nurses from health. You may already have had contact with social services or be receiving a service from them at present. Social services departments are also involved in fostering and adoption. Some of our work with parents and carers is with foster and adoptive parents who have positively sought a child with learning disabilities to be part of their family. Social and health services are also involved in providing staffed accommodation and personal support, and these are also in what is called the independent or non-statutory sector. Housing associations, charitable bodies and not-for-profit organisations are becoming involved in housing and personal support services for adults with learning disabilities. Disability organisations such as Mencap and the National Autistic Society are also involved here. Children with learning disabilities are mainly the responsibility of education and social services departments. Courses at colleges of further education are increasingly becoming a 'bridge' between child-centred services and those for adults. In recent years there has been a growth in social and leisure opportunities for people with learning disabilities, some of which are largely separate from ordinary activities and take place in, say, the local leisure centre, but others make a positive attempt to integrate with whatever is going on in the community.

Accepting the rightness and reality of people with learning disabilities as sexual beings is a huge challenge to all these agencies and one that can no longer be 'ducked'. Apart from the importance of truly valuing people with learning disabilities and working with them in a respectful way, all service agencies must create and nurture structures and attitudes that are able to respond appropriately within this crucial area. Each agency or service has its own specific role and involvement in the lives of people with learning disabilities and often their families. Because sexuality is integral to all human life, activity and relationships it must be an issue for them. When dealing with matters of sexuality, an organisation will usually adopt either a re-active, or a pro-active approach. If they are faced with a problem that can't be dodged – an all-too-common example is of a person's inappropriate sexual behaviour – the question has to be asked: 'What can we do?' The solution tends to be short term, pragmatic and local: that is, only the particular, immediate issue is dealt with. A more visionary approach – the pro-active one – will take a long-term view of how things should be, 'if only', and seeks to develop a strategy or battle plan, because, inevitably, many people have to be convinced and converted. Much of our work is advising and responding to the re-active approach. This is unavoidable, given the poor history associated with people with learning disabilities as sexual beings and the relative newness of this subject. There are benefits, however; it means that plans for the future can be based on the understanding of why things are still so difficult now.

GETTING TO GRIPS WITH SEXUALITY ISSUES

If any agency or organisation is seriously to get to grips with sexuality issues it needs to consider the following.

The place of parents
In Chapter 5, we looked at how necessary it is for professionals to consult, involve and work with parents, and to do so in a way that views them positively as equal partners in the relationship.

The complexities of this subject
As a parent you know only too well that there seem to be so many 'opposites' to make sense of: there is a continuing tussle between protecting and risk taking; an apparent gulf between your views and those of others, especially professionals; the range from very able to profound in the disability spectrum, which makes a vital difference in making sense of sexuality – some people with learning disabilities do have good information and meaningful choices in their lives, whilst others have little of these; some can advocate effectively for themselves, others are not yet able to or, if they can, are not listened to. Rights, empowerment and the reality of vulnerability, have to be weighed and considered both in a general and a particular way for each person with learning disabilities in order to achieve the best possible outcome; there is the reality of sexual abuse and there are people who don't believe it happens; there is evidence of sexuality and sexual feelings in a person with learning disabilities, and there is the parent who finds that hard to face, or denies it altogether. And caught between these different perspectives, these conflicting realities is the person with learning disabilities.

Agencies too must recognise these differing viewpoints and not be overwhelmed by them. It is usually from professionals that solutions to difficulties or ways through complexities are sought so understanding and steady realism are vital. For instance, when agencies (and others) resort to a re-active approach, they need to acknowledge that change and improvement for a person with learning disabilities are likely to happen very slowly. A harder reality is that, for some people, change may never happen, because their needs are so great, and the resources required to meet them so significant and continuing, that they can't be provided. In such a situation it's best for the agency to be realistic and honest about this and concentrate on ensuring that the caring environment is as respectful and understanding as can be achieved. It may do more harm than good if an agency is not realistic, for example, by starting something that can't be sustained. It can only be realistic if it is fully aware of the complexity of the various strands and how they interlink. Let's return to Darren (see Chapter 8). If, after six months, the manager does decide that the work must stop, what is the likely consequence? Staff may still have to manage his behaviour, which may get worse. Darren, too, is left with the practical realities of such behaviour, and, furthermore, the emotional consequences of having his learning and behavioural needs unmet. Everyone will continue to struggle.

It might have been better had nothing started in the first place: Darren will be hurt and confused to have the one-to-one attention of the worker withdrawn, especially if it is not 'explained' in a way he can understand – and the chances are it can't be.

If the manager of Darren's day centre were realistic and aware from the start, (s)he might not have agreed to any one-to-one work being done for the reasons given.

The need for policies and guidelines
Both policies and guidelines are crucial for staff and people with learning disabilities. The purpose of a policy is to state the organisation's attitudes and beliefs towards the subject or issue in question. The purpose of guidelines is to make it clear to staff how they are to behave in their professional capacities. So guidelines for a Policy on Personal Relationships, Sexuality and People with Learning Disabilities might include rights and responsibilities, staff attitudes, staff responsibilities, sexual activity, appropriate and inappropriate touch, parents and carers' involvement, sexual preference, contraception, marriage and parenthood, for example.

Other guidelines would be needed for certain specialist issues, such as people with learning disabilities and with mental health needs, whose behaviour is moving towards sexually offending, thus putting themselves and others at risk. Apart from policies and guidelines such as Personal Relationships and Sexuality, agencies should have relevant documents on the following areas: protection, sexuality work, risk management, intimate care, whistle blowing, and also have clear complaints procedures. In all, they should provide a clear, comprehensive approach, based on a well thought out set of beliefs and values. Policies and guidelines benefit staff as well as service users. They make clear what is expected of staff and, equally vital, what constitutes good practice. It is, therefore, much harder for indifferent attitudes and poor practice to be tolerated.

Good policies and guidelines offer reassurance to parents, by making clear what they can expect from the services provided for their child regarding standards of provision and responses should things not go well.

It's worth saying that policies and guidelines can only be enhanced by parents being involved in the drawing-up process – being consulted individually and in groups; perhaps being part of the group who writes them. People with learning disabilities should also be involved in this process, which should ensure that their contribution is made as meaningful as possible.

Staff recruitment and training

Any respectable agency should make sure that applicants for vacant posts are introduced to its policies. This is especially important in the areas of sexuality and vulnerability, where prejudice and failure to understand their significance may risk what the service is trying to achieve. It immediately gives a message that the agency is serious about the subject of sexuality and protection, and also clear about what it expects from its staff. Those newly appointed should spend part of their induction period becoming familiar with the policies and guidelines, and be given opportunities to talk these through with an appropriate person, so that when they start work 'proper' they are clear about what's expected of and from them.

For staff already in post, training is essential so that they can become familiar and comfortable with the documents. By this we mean all staff – cooks, domestics and drivers, as well as managers and care staff. Think back to the Rights we talked about in Chapter 6 and particularly the one: 'not to be at the mercy of the sexual attitudes of individual care givers'. It's only too easy for other people, for all kinds of reasons, to undermine or otherwise jeopardise good and respectful work being done. By participating in training all staff receive the message that their attitudes have an important influence on those they work with, and, therefore, that their role in the lives of people with learning disabilities does matter.

Training is also an important way of maintaining consistency, so that one positive comment or attitude is not undermined by something entirely contradictory and inappropriate.

Policies and guidelines should be reviewed periodically in the light of continuing practice. A mechanism needs to be set up by which this is done. Certainly staff training is one useful way in which practice feedback can be obtained. Monitoring and reviewing ensures that policies and guidelines are 'living' documents, responsive to changing circumstances and improving practice.

Sexuality work

This was discussed in the previous chapter. If you believe that a service which your son or daughter is receiving could do more with regard to sexuality work, then you may need to think about some questions to put to them in order to get the discussion going.

Agencies working together

Where sexuality and protecting people with learning disabilities are concerned, consistency is vital. It's no good a person being told one thing by a professional or agency, and the exact opposite by another. Most people with learning disabilities are known to a number of different services. Let's take Miriam and Ajay as examples.

Miriam

Miriam goes to a mainstream secondary school with her own support assistant. Transport is provided by a taxi and she has an escort. One weekend each month, Miriam goes to Hannah and Geoff, who are her share care family. On Wednesday evenings she attends a leisure club run by her local authority recreation service. At the age of 14 she has been allocated a social worker from the Children's Disability Team to help plan for her eventual transition from school.

Ajay

Ajay lives in a group home with two other people. Together they receive a certain amount of personal care and domestic support. He also attends a nearby horticultural project which provides work experience for people with learning disabilities. Currently, Ajay is visited by a social worker from the Community Team for Learning Disabilities. Once a month he enjoys walking as part of a range of leisure opportunities organised jointly by social services and recreation, of which volunteers are an essential part.

Within the lives of Miriam and Ajay are many different people, lay and professional, each with their own opinions and beliefs on sexuality and vulnerability. If their respective agencies have clear policies and guidelines, confusion and ambiguity will be kept to a minimum. This applies as much to volunteers as to paid workers. It is also important that each agency's policies and guidelines are compatible, ideally with each one signing up to the one comprehensive document. Realistically, at this stage, that is unlikely, but nevertheless it is a principle to aim for.

Social services departments and health trusts have a key role to play in recognising the importance of consistency. Not only do they provide direct services themselves, they also buy-in services from other agencies. These may be from other statutory bodies, but are more likely to be from the independent sector – that is, voluntary organisations, charities and for profit/not-for-profit organisations. There has been a significant increase in this area of service provision in recent years, particularly for adults with learning disabilities. Social services departments and health authorities, as purchasers or commissioners of services, are well placed to ask questions of potential providers about their policy towards valuing people with learning disabilities, their rights as sexual beings and their right to be protected from any harm. As a matter of good practice we would hope a negative answer would mean that service is rejected in favour of one that has already got to grips with the issue, or is at least on the way to doing so. We have come across a number of small independent services which see that they have gaps in this area and are taking steps to rectify that, which is encouraging. Recognising the need is the first of those steps. But if the statutory authority, in its powerful commissioning role, is not asking the questions, then a great opportunity for improvement is being missed.

Developing a vision or strategy within a geographical area

This continues the last point. One way in which agencies can work together in an area is by setting up a forum or meeting place. Here individuals representing either themselves (as parent or person with a learning disability) or an organisation (voluntary, statutory or parents' group) meet regularly to share their views, ideas and experiences. From this sharing there should emerge a vision, or dream, about how sexuality and protection can be organised and managed in the best possible way for all concerned. Then the hard work begins! The task of the forum is to work on a strategy, or design, as to how this vision can be achieved. We've already discussed some of these elements – policies and guidelines, service commissioning, sexuality work, staff training, respectful partnerships involving professionals, parents and people with learning disabilities, what constitutes good practice – there will be many others. It will work best if the forum is part of an existing planning structure, because then it has influence and can feed into the service planning process.

Forum membership should ideally be a mix of policy makers, managers and practitioners who, together with parents and people with learning disabilities, will be a powerful combination, provided people work together in mutual respect. As well as sharing, discussing and learning locally, a forum could also look outward, to other areas of the country (other countries?) in order to learn from their experiences. If good practice exists in one place, it makes sense for that to be shared elsewhere. If some information, knowledge, expertise, idea etc. is held in one place, then others need to know where to find it. Organisations, such as those listed at the end of this book, can make a significant difference to individuals' lives and improving services. However, in spite of their best efforts, some of these organisations are not so well known as they need to be. Again, an important role for a forum would be to build up a resource bank of useful information that could be tapped into. There is an initiative called 'It's Only Natural' which is available to work with groups and agencies in distinct geographical areas. A key outcome of its work is two one-day conferences – one for parents, the other for professionals – from which will develop a forum for the interested parties in that area.

Not all organisations locally may at first recognise the importance of this subject or the possibilities offered by a forum, but as time passes, they may see that not being involved is to be left out! Many services today are under great pressure to deliver as efficiently as possible. There may be a struggle to maintain resource levels, to cope with increasing expectations and responsibilities (as within schools). Just keeping afloat with providing the service may be an achievement without having to take on something as specific and hard as sexuality issues. How can services be persuaded to go that little bit further, and see sexuality as more than an add-on issue: as absolutely integral to the lives of those with whom they work?

10　What you might do next

In this final chapter we aim to harness all the energy that we hope the book has generated in you to bring about some of the changes that you might be hoping are possible. So we make two different suggestions for courses of action you might take. There may be others that occur to you. The two we suggest are very different in approach, although the action plan – the suggested series of steps you could take – basically works well with either. The first approach primarily uses the imagination; the other is more of a logical, thinking process.

DREAMING THE DREAM

This is something you can do now, or leave until you are where you do your best thinking, such as in the bath, out walking or even in bed at three o'clock in the morning! To start with, we would like you to 'daydream', or imagine for a while, how things would look if they were as good as they could be for your son or daughter . . . This may mean a little bit of fantasising, so the picture that comes to you may seem unachievable. That doesn't matter, because there may be something on the way to that picture that is possible.

> 'When Debbie lived with her mum, she used to come and stay with us for a week or so. We would go window-shopping sometimes, and try to get her to say which trousers or shoes she liked the look of. It was like getting blood from a stone; she would always say, "I don't know, which ones do you like?" I coped with this by visualising her going out with friends and coming home with something

> *nice she'd chosen for herself. Now, ten years later, Debbie*
> *lives with us. She does exactly this; in fact she's a lot better*
> *dressed than we are!'*
>
> Eve

Debbie's new life has come about partly because of circumstances, but Frank, Eve's husband, says that, unless they had
been able to visualise a better way for Debbie, then little would
have changed.

> *'I would like Stuart to have a partner. He is interested in*
> *girls. I would like him to experience a loving sexual*
> *relationship that is appropriate for him.'*
>
> Judith

In order to move *your* 'dream' or 'picture' from your imagination into reality, what needs to happen? It partly depends on what
you have visualised; as we can see, Eve's and Judith's 'dreams'
are very different. What is true is that by having a clear picture
of what could be, the first step has already been taken towards
making it a reality, however unrealistic it may appear. And it's
OK to stay with that first step, thinking about it and nurturing it.
Maybe the time hasn't yet come when you should be taking
action. However, if you do want to take the second step, these
are some of the things you might want to consider in terms of an
action plan:

- Even if your 'dream' is way in the future – for example, Judith
  visualises Stuart as an adult in a loving sexual relationship, but
  he is only 13 – there are still many steps that can be taken in
  order to make that 'dream' more possible. So, Judith could
  consider the following – what more does Stuart need to know
  (that is, in terms of further information and appropriate
  experiences)? Does he have sufficient opportunity to develop
  friendships with others of his own age? What local services
  exist to support him in adulthood towards independence? How
  can his self-esteem be further enhanced? Even if the prospect
  of Stuart being able to cope with and sustain a loving sexual
  relationship is improbable, the steps that Judith could take
  below are all entirely appropriate. This would encourage him,

and his carers if necessary, to make the most of his potential as he moves into adulthood and the possibility for a fulfilling life becomes clearer.

- Do you need to be talking to someone else at this stage about either the 'dream' or the next step to take? If so, who is that person? It could be a close relative, friend, another parent, a trusted professional or possibly your daughter or son – depending on the 'dream' and your circumstances. You'll know best about that. Talking or sharing with another person can be an excellent way of shrinking anxieties and fears and expanding our hopes. Other people may see possibilities that we (in our reservations) cannot.
- Think about some of the questions and points you want to put to key people, especially those who are in positions of influence and power. Remember that, as a parent, you have the right to raise any concerns, and make any points that matter to you and to your child's future.
- Make alliances, gather around you the people who can understand your 'dream' and help it become reality. Very often this will be other parents whose situations are similar to yours. There can be great strength in numbers.
- If your 'dream' is way in the future or seems unachievable at the moment, that's OK. For all sorts of reasons there may be no action to take at present. In the meantime just keeping in touch with the 'picture' will be powerful in itself and maybe sufficient to sustain you.
- Anything you may think of that we haven't.

PERSONAL REVIEW

In your mind think about all the services your son or daughter receives – school/college/day placement, short break/shared care; leisure activities etc. – how do you think they rate as far as sexuality and protection are concerned? Where there are real successes or achievements, give praise where it's due. By looking at how and why something has worked, good practice can be transferred elsewhere. And acknowledging good practice certainly encourages it to continue. However, if there are areas of concern or anxiety, pinpoint what these are; try and be clear about the gaps you see. If you have an intuitive sense of unease, then try to nail it in your own mind as far as you can. Certainly trust that sense, even if it is hard to pin down at this stage.

When you've taken that as far as you can, move through the steps mentioned above. If any action at present is not appropriate, maybe it's a question of simply digesting what's been said.

Whatever your circumstances, we hope that reading this book has proved worth while for you. It is certainly not the last word on the subject although we ourselves have to find 'last words' to say here; perhaps these should be that sexuality and sexuality work with people who have learning disabilities are still too often seen as the 'icing on the cake,' a luxury afforded only to a few. There needs to be a move from that position to another where sexuality and sexuality work are put at the heart of people's lives, be they child or adult, and seen for what they really are – not just the icing, but the cake itself. We offer this book as a contribution to this process. Maybe you too could be a part of that move.

Useful organisations

Respond
3rd Floor, 24/32 Stephenson Way
London NW1 2HD
Tel: 020 7383 0700
*(Challenges vulnerability and
sexual abuse in the lives of
people with learning disabilities.
Telephone Helpline – 0845–606–
1503 – available for people with
learning disabilities, parents,
carers and professionals on
issues of sexual abuse, sexual
offending and related behaviours)*

Ann Craft Trust (ACT)
Centre for Social Work
University of Nottingham
University Park
Nottingham NG7 2RD
Tel: 0115 951 5400
*(For advice and support for
professionals working in the area
of rights/protection/sexuality and
people with learning disabilities)*

NAZ Project London
Palingswick House
241 King Street
London W6 9LP
Tel: 020 8741 1879
*(For advice regarding sexual
health issues specifically for
people from Muslim and the
South Asian communities)*

**Family Planning Association
(FPA)**
2–12 Pentonville Road
London N1 9FP
Tel 020 7837 5432

Pavilion Publishing
8 St George's Place
Brighton BN1 4ZZ
Tel: 01273 623222
*(Distributes a wide range of
resources on issues relating to
people with learning disabilities)*

People First
Instrument House
207–215 Kings Cross Road
London WC1X 9DD
Tel: 020 7713 6400
*(A self-advocacy group run by
and for people with learning
difficulties. Groups exist in many
other places)*

Discern
Chadburn House
Weighbridge Road
Littleworth
Mansfield NG18 1AH
Tel: 01623 623732
*(Offers counselling for disabled
people on personal relationships
and sexuality)*

Voice UK
PO Box 238
Derby DE1 9JN
Tel: 01332 202555
*(The voice of people with
learning disabilities who have
experienced crime or abuse)*

**Association for Residential
Care**
ARC House
Marsden Street
Chesterfield S4O 1JY
Tel: 01246 555043
*(A national umbrella
organisation which exists to
promote the quality of life,
maintenance of standards and
diversity of residential and day
services for people with LD)*

**The Association to Aid the
Sexual and Personal
Relationships of People with a
Disability (SPOD)**
286 Camden Road
London NT 0BJ
Tel: 020 7607 8851
*(Counselling and/or advice
available for anyone with a
disability, experiencing sexual or
relationship difficulties.
Professionals and carers may
also contact direct)*

Protective Behaviours
(Jocelyn Rose)
Health Improvement Team
Shipley Court
Marsh End Road
Milton Keynes MK16 8EA
Tel: 01908 217121

Protection Portfolio
Connect at Barnardo's
Queens House, Queens Road
Bradford BD8 7BS
Tel: 01274 481183

Values Incorporated
(Simon Goldsmith)
596 Rollo Road
Hexstable
Kent BR8 7RD
Tel: 01322 614659
*(An independent training and
development service, working
mostly with agencies in London
and the South East. It undertakes
consultancy and project work in
a variety of areas, including the
development of community and
primary care services. It has a
particular interest in supporting
disabled people and carers to
plan for the future and access
the services they need)*

**Your local Community Team
for Learning Disabilities**
Contact via your Social Services
Department

It's Only Natural
Sue Blackwell
Pogstone House
19 Cuckstool Road
Denby Dale
Huddersfield HD8 8RF
Tel: 01484 861854
*(A parent-led initiative aimed at
establishing sexuality and
learning disability forums in
different geographical areas)*

Consent
Woodside Road
Abbots Langley
Herts WD5 0HT
Tel: 01923 670796
(Offers a range of services in response to various sexuality issues regarding people with learning disabilities)

Your local Health Promotion Service

Circles Network
Parnwell House
160 Pennywell Road
Upper Easton
Bristol BS5 0TX
Tel: 0117 939 3917

Connect
Barnardo's Queens Road Project
Queens House, Queens Road
Bradford BD8 7BS
Tel: 01274 481183
(Provides advice, training and support on sexuality, protection and people with learning disabilities in the Yorkshire area, and elsewhere as time permits. Also involved in a number of development initiatives)

References

BEWLEY, C. (1998). *Choice and Control.* Values Into Action, Oxford House, Derbyshire Street, London E2 6HG.

BROWN, H. and TURK, V. (1994). Social Care Research Findings, 46.

BROWN, H. and TURK, V. (1995). 'The Sexual Abuse of Adults with Learning Disabilities: Report of a Second Two-Year Incidence Survey.' In *Mental Handicap Research*, 8, 1.

CROSS, M. (1998). *Proud Child, Safer Child.* Women's Press Handbook Series.

DEPARTMENT OF HEALTH (2000). *No Secrets: Guidance on Developing and Implementing Multi-agency Policies and Procedures to Protect Vulnerable Adults from Abuse.*

GASCOIGNE, E. (1995). *Working with Parents as Partners in SEN.* David Fulton Publishers, London.

GIBRAN, K. (1926). *The Prophet.* Heinemann. Now available from Pan Books.

KITSON, D. and LIVINGSTONE, J. (1998). *The Day We Found Her Crying.* ARC, ARC House, Marsden Street, Chesterfield, S40 1JY.

LAW SOCIETY (1998). 'Who Decides?' Response to the Consultation Paper issued by the Lord Chancellor's Department, London. Quoted in *Choice and Control*, (1998). Bewley, C. Values Into Action.

MAKSYM, D. (1990). *Shared Feelings.* The G. Allan Roeher Institute, Kinsmen Building, York University, 4700 Keele Street, North York, Ontario, Canada M3J 1P3.

NOLAN, CHRISTOPHER (1987). *Under the Eye of the Clock.* Weidenfeld & Nicolson.

ROBINSON, C. and STALKER, K. (1998). *Growing Up With Disability.* Jessica Kingsley Publishers.

SINASON, V. (1992). *Mental Handicap and the Human Condition*. Free Association, London.

WALSH, B. (1994). *How to set up trusts and user controlled independent living schemes*. Independent Living Network of Tower Hamlets, London.